This Is Hockey

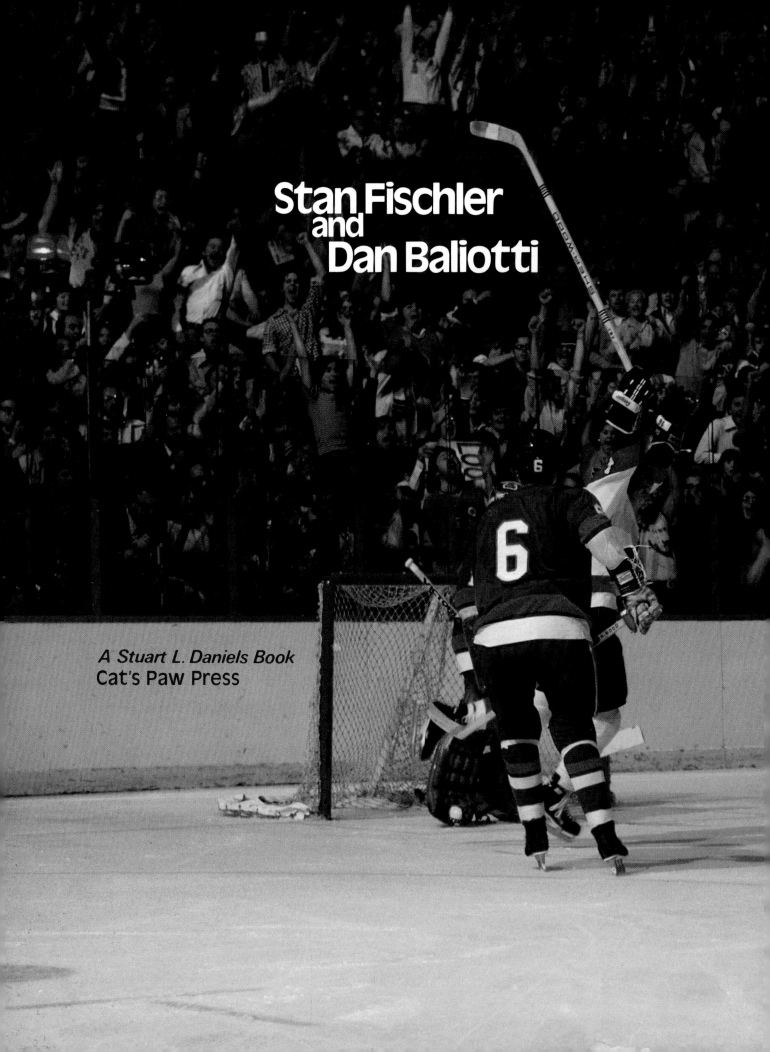

Stan Fischler
and
Dan Baliotti

A Stuart L. Daniels Book
Cat's Paw Press

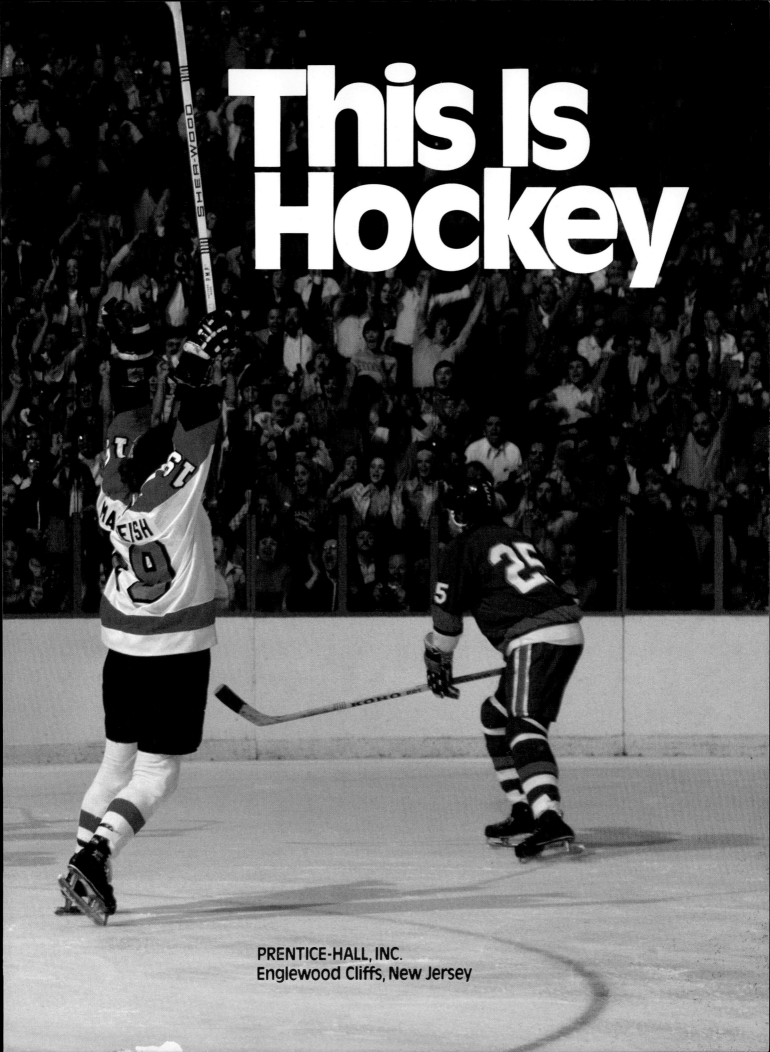

This Is Hockey

PRENTICE-HALL, INC.
Englewood Cliffs, New Jersey

THIS IS HOCKEY
by Stan Fischler and Dan Baliotti

Copyright © 1975 by
Cat's Paw Press, Inc.

A Stuart L. Daniels Book
Published by Prentice-Hall, Inc.
Englewood Cliffs, New Jersey

Printed in the United States of America T
Prentice-Hall International, Inc., London
Prentice-Hall of Australia, Pty. Ltd., Sydney
Prentice-Hall of Canada, Ltd., Toronto
Prentice-Hall of India Private Ltd., New Delhi
Prentice-Hall of Japan, Inc., Tokyo

Library of Congress Catalog Card Number: 75-15440

ISBN: 0-13-919142-9

Contents

Hockey-
A War Game on Ice

Professional hockey is a war game played on ice.

Each contest is a battle whose often well planned strategy draws upon the most sophisticated technology to produce victory.

As in war, hockey battles result in bloodshed. Hockey has its "no man's land" and it has its trenches. "There," says Philadelphia Flyers' coach Fred Shero, "is where the punishment is dealt. It doesn't matter how big or flashy a guy is. If he can't go in and battle, he should join the Ice Follies."

"In other sports a star can avoid his share of punishment by going out-of-bounds. The beauty of hockey as a test of courage is that there is no out-of-bounds."

The art of throwing body against body is sanctioned and often encouraged in hockey. "If you can't beat 'em in the alley, you can't beat 'em on the ice" is a cherished bromide of the sport. It is important to believe fully in hand-to-hand combat.

That, in part, explains why the Philadelphia Flyers were the champions of the National Hockey League in 1974 and 1975. They battled all the way. They also knew the combat zones better than their opponents. They won the battles of the face-offs and the challenge of the four corners of the rink. At other times, as one critic observed, "They were graceless bullies who replaced the ballet of their sport with a new theater of brutality."

But hockey and the Flyers are more than that. The game also has its noblemen—knights who fight the ice war as if artistry and chivalry are all that mattered.

The lyrical skating of players like Gil Perreault of the Buffalo Sabres has all the grace one sees in the movements of Rudolf Nureyev performing a ballet. And when the Canadiens execute one of their pattern passing movements the ice becomes a chessboard.

It is in the skating that the true beauty of hockey is found. Hockey without skates says one longtime lover of the game would have nothing to recommend it. It would have all the fan appeal of broomball. Skating is to hockey what bubbles are to champagne.

But the other components are just as vital—the glory, the heartbreak, the violence, the one-on-one challenge of shooter against goaltender and the absolute masculinity of it all. Woven throughout is the Canadian character. For hockey, born in the cold climes of Ontario and Quebec, originally was Canada's game. The imprint of the rugged Canadian remains to this day. But hockey is now worldwide. It is fast becoming international in character.

"There's the muscularity of it," writes Canadian author Dennis Braithwaite, "the need for bruising body contact action, simpleminded love of winning, toughness and zest masked by taciturnity,

9

Left: *This is worth fighting for. Bobby Clarke, captain of the Philadelphia Flyers, reflects the ecstasy that hockey players have experienced over the years when the coveted Stanley Cup was won.*

impatience, eagerness, thirst for simple solutions and the underlying anti-intellectualism."

In its basic form hockey has not changed since it was invented by Canadians in the 19th century. Winning teams, such as the Philadelphia Flyers, the Montreal Canadiens and the Boston Bruins, capture their championships just as superior clubs did in the late eighteen hundreds with competent goaltenders, a rock-ribbed defense and high-powered scorers.

In the United States sports enthusiasts have come to adopt and love the game. From Boston to Atlanta, from Broadway to Beverly Hills, Americans have developed a taste for the frosty speed and exhilarating crash bang of hockey.

The point counterpoint that occurs between artistry and violence remains the constant. And always, the war theme. The players are the warriors. As one observer noted, "They provide the essential catharsis for frustrated clerks, failed athletes and paunchy businessmen."

Hockey is played by aristocrats and non-aristocrats at Harvard, by youngsters in prep schools and high schools across the land, by black kids in the Harlem ghetto and even by inmates at the Joyceville Penitentiary in Kingston, Ontario.

They all play because within each contestant's mind is the dream of becoming another Bobby Clarke—Bobby Clarke who came down from Flin Flon, Manitoba, on the edge of the Arctic Circle, to help win the Stanley Cup—or a Rod Gilbert or a Bobby Hull or a Bobby Orr.

"When I got to the NHL," Clarke recalls, "every game was a dream come true for me. I was playing against all the people I had watched as a kid on TV. I could actually line up against them and see just how good I really was."

As in war, hockey has the exhilaration of triumph and the despair of defeat. Reggie Fleming played on the Chicago Black Hawks' last Stanley Cup winning team in 1961 and then served with the Bruins, the Rangers and other NHL teams. He scaled the heights and then plummeted to the depths of despair. In 1974, he found himself being treated like a raw rookie when he reported for duty with the now defunct Chicago Cougars.

"I played pro hockey for eighteen years," says Fleming, "and when I came back for the 19th year they gave me a try-out form. If they don't know

what I can do after 18 years then they can go to hell. Still," he says proudly, "I get respect, because they know I'm Reggie Fleming."

He played for 18 years in the *front lines*. He *has* to get respect.

For every Reggie Fleming who goes down, there's a kid like Mike Kitchen climbing to the top. In 1975 Kitchen skated for the Toronto Marlboros who won the Memorial Cup. It symbolizes the Junior championship of Canada, the teenagers' Stanley Cup.

"Hey, you mean we really won?" shouted teammate John Anderson in the steamy dressing room after the conquest in May 1975. "Maybe I'll wake up tomorrow and the Memorial Cup won't be there." Then a pause, "Maybe this'll finally get us some cheers in school."

A listener chimed in, "It's a cinch to get you a pro contract."

"Or at least broads," another teammate laughed.

As the Detroit Red Wings seek to gain some of the glory they enjoyed in bygone years, forward Nick Libett has become one of the most important skaters in their renaissance.

When it comes to the care and repair of their equipment, few athletes are as sensitive as hockey players. They are most concerned about their skates. The razor thin blades need constant attention from the team trainer whose job it is to be certain that the blades are in perfect condition for quick stops and starts. The trainer uses a special skate sharpener for this purpose.

Few spectacles in sport can match the pageantry of an international hockey match between European and North American skaters. One of the most pulsating moments occurred prior to the game between Team Canada 1974 and the Soviet National Team at Maple Leaf Gardens in Toronto. The players are lined up for the Canadian National Anthem. The Russians are to the left and Team Canada is at the opposite end of the rink.

The road to the top, however, is strewn with land mines, and their impact is the progenitor of anguish. During the 1975 Stanley Cup play-offs the New York Islanders' leading scorer, Bob Nystrom, suffered through 41 shots without scoring a goal. After Philadelphia had beaten his team for the third straight game, Nystrom glanced at his right arm. Small red blotches had appeared above his wrist. "Hives," he said. "I think this is really starting to get to me."

Just three games later the Islanders tied the series in what has gone down in the annals of the game as a monumental upset. Nystrom had finally scored, goaltender Glenn "Chico" Resch had become the newest hero and the once proud Flyers teetered on the brink of collapse.

This was the Flyers' Stalingrad. And, like the Russians in World War II, they rallied. They used skill, strategy and an unusual mystical power unknown in any other sport. They imported Miss Kate Smith, the vocalist, the Philadelphia Flyers' special hockey good luck charm.

Only in hockey would a Kate Smith perform magic. But she did, transporting 17,000 Philadelphia Spectrum fans into wild fits of joy as she sang "God Bless America" before the final game against the Islanders. Her record is almost flawless. In the times she has sung that stirring anthem in person or recorded, the Flyers have won forty-four out of forty-seven games.

Her magic helped beat the Islanders that day. When the Flyers were tied two games each with the Buffalo Sabres in the Stanley Cup finals, Kate's recording of "God Bless America" was rolled into place like a crucial piece of artillery. Philadelphia won and marched to its second Stanley Cup in a row.

More than any other competitive sport, hockey stirs the most intense emotions among participants, coaches, fans and owners alike.

It is also a sport of such beauty and artistry that the world renowned Russian poet Yevgeny Yevtushenko after watching a Boston Bruins' game waxed ecstatic over scoring ace Phil Esposito.

"He [Esposito] is the poet," said Yevtushenko. "The farmer who loves the earth, the hunter who loves the forest, the seaman who loves the sea, they are poets. Esposito loves it on the ice. Therefore, he is a poet."

Some hockey players, themselves, view the game as an existential experience. The simple act of skating infuses them with a "high" that only they can describe. Former NHL forward Eric Nesterenko once relayed his thoughts to author Studs Terkel and they appear in Terkel's book, *Working*.

A lanky, long-legged skater, Nesterenko revelled in the feel of crossing leg over leg as he accelerated up the ice:

I haven't kept many photographs of myself but I found one where I'm in full flight. I'm leaning into a turn. You pick up the centrifugal forces and you lay into it. For a few seconds, like a gyroscope, they support you. I'm concentrating on something and I'm grinning. That's the way I like to picture myself.

A clash of titans. Bobby Orr (No. 4) and Brad Park have been among the NHL's best offensive defensemen in the seventies. Orr is trying to outrace Park for a loose puck in the corner of the rink, as goalie Gilles Villemure looks on.

I'm something else there. I'm on another level of existence, just being in pure motion. Going wherever I want to. That's nice, you know.

A few days after the Flyers won the Stanley Cup in 1975 more than two million fans cheered them. Philadelphia's victory parade was led by Bobby Clarke. At the time he was the boyish looking twenty-five year old, five-foot-ten Clarke. But with his toothless grin he was not the usual swooning material. His teammate, star goalie Bernie Parent, looks more like a bartender than a superstar. Hardly swooning material either. Yet they swooned. "Bern-Nee! Bern-Nee!" came the shouts as goaltender Bernie Parent stood upon a float and waved to the crowd. When Parent took brief leave for an emergency visit to a nearby neighborhood toilet to relieve himself, Philadelphians recommended that the urinal hereafter be designated a municipal shrine!

What is the reason for all of this? The more real a figure is, psychologists explain, the more the person next door likes him and finds opportunities for forming affection for him. Hockey players are real that way.

Coach Fred Shero also rode at the front of the tumultuous victory parade for two years in a row. But he knew that the following year—or any year—could be different. "You know," he has said, "success is like a shooting star. It comes and goes very fast. It could be gone tomorrow."

A hero today—tomorrow, who knows? Emotions ranging from high to low are felt by hockey players every year. For Bill Clement of the champion Flyers, the downer came just days after he had revelled in the grand victory parade. General manager Keith Allen phoned to tell Clement he had been dealt from the very top to the very bottom club, to the last place Washington Capitals.

"When the phone call came," says Clement, "it was very upsetting. It will take a long time to get over the emotional upheaval. It was one of my unhappiest days because I had to leave everything I had learned to love."

There are other downers. Watching an expert goalie such as Bernie Parent stop sure goal after sure goal demoralizes the enemy. "God couldn't have made all the saves that Parent made against us," said Buffalo defenseman Jerry Korab after the 1975 play-offs.

Once a forward skates around his foe it is difficult for the checking player to snare the puck from him.

Watching your team play through an 80-game schedule with the sun shining on them and then suddenly fall under a black cloud when play-off elimination occurs inspires different emotions in different people. It has happened many times for Rangers' manager Emile Francis.

"It's a tough business," says Francis, "but when you've been in this business as long as I have, you see the good days and the bad days. You learn to accept both. If you can't, you'd better get out of it.

"The way I've always operated, when you get knocked on your bottom, you've got to pick yourself up, roll up your sleeves and go back to work again. What you don't do is hide in the closet. Sure it's hard . . . but you've got to be hard."

Bruins' manager Harry Sinden knows how hard a man must be in the professional game. He, too, has won—and lost. In April 1975 his powerful Boston team was upset by the Chicago Black Hawks. It was one of the worst downers in Sinden's life.

"Everybody was upset," says Sinden, "because nobody expected it would happen. A guy from the Boston Celtics—a friend of mine—told me that they [the press] were cutting us up. Well, I didn't expect anything different. Everybody's gotta get a kick at the cat."

For others, the downer is more personal and serious. The unsung heroines of hockey are the players' wives, who come to the arenas week in and week out and watch in joy and sadness as their husbands win and lose. From time to time, they watch in utter horror as their loved ones are injured.

In January 1968 Carol Masterton was seated at the Metropolitan Sports Center in Bloomington, Minnesota, as her husband Bill skated for the North Stars in a relatively routine game against the Oakland Seals. Bill carried the puck to the enemy blue line and attempted to split a defense comprised of Larry Cahan and Ron Harris, two notoriously hard but clean body checkers.

"I was watching him," Carol Masterton related, "because he was my husband. He appeared to just come over the blue line and make the pass. Then he appeared to go up in the air. His feet kind of went straight out from under him and he went right down on his head."

Bill Masterton never regained consciousness. He suffered a head injury, went into a coma and

15

died shortly thereafter. "I've never felt any bitterness against hockey," said Carol Masterton. "Bill played the game because he loved it."

That special frenzy, that utter madness that hockey produces in its fans is brought about by a distillation of speed, blood, science and luck. It is what results in characters like Dutchie Van Eden.

For those to whom the excitement of ice hockey has become an almost mystical experience, their loyalty and/or disdain knows no boundaries. There is no more dedicated sports fan than a hockey enthusiast.

Dutchie came to Montreal from Holland in 1957 and within a few years established himself as the number one fan of the Montreal Canadiens. But it is not enough to say simply that Dutchie is a fan; he is a one-man hockey vaudeville show who visits the Forum with a seven dollar megaphone painted red, white and blue, the Canadiens' colors, and shouts, "Go Habs, Go!" at the top of his lungs.

That's just for starters. From his station in the aisle of Section 10-12 Dutchie delivers a commentary for every occasion.

"WAAAHAAAAAA! Sob! Sniffle! BOO-HOOOOOAaa!" That's Dutchie's Bronx cheer when the other team gets a penalty. "I give it to the guy in the box," says Dutchie. "Especially guys like Phil Esposito who are always whining. It really shakes some guys up. You can see them looking up at the seats trying to find the baby. Hah!"

Then there is the ear-shattering: "Huh-huh-HOO-hoo! Huh-huh-HOO-hoo! Huh-huh-huh-huh-huh!" Dutchie uses that specialty—he calls it Woody Woodpecker—when the Canadiens are shorthanded and successfully ice the puck. "I'm sort of making fun of the other teams, you know, like 'Hey, you stupid dummies, can't ya do anything?'"

There is a Dutchie in every city and town where hockey is played. And every one of them in one way or another shares Dutchie's sentiments when he says, "When I die, I want to be buried under the ice at the Forum so I can hear them skating above me."

For those on the actual firing line the combat experience cannot be duplicated. For goalie Glenn Resch the night of April 24, 1975 will never be forgotten. That was the night he beat the Penguins in a Stanley Cup game and for the first time in his life kissed the goalpost.

There were five minutes and twenty-seven seconds left in the first period. Ron Schock of the Penguins shot the puck from fifteen feet and the puck was a blur as it whistled low past Resch's stick. The shot struck the left goalpost and spun away from the goal area through the crease. It saved the Islanders. Resch turned and saw what had happened. He knelt by the metal pipe that had saved him and pursed his lips through his face mask. "I would have given that goalpost a great big hug if I'd had time." Later, the Islanders skated off with the win.

Goaltending drives some men almost crazy. "It's a rough job," says Sabres' goalie Gerry Desjardins. "If I were starting all over again I wouldn't be a goaltender. It's driven a lot of guys out of the game, out of their minds."

During the 1975 season Cesare Maniago of the Minnesota North Stars pulled himself out of a game long before it was over. "He didn't say a word," said a teammate. "He just skated off the ice, past the bench and into the dressing room."

A few months later, Desjardins did virtually the same thing in one of the final games against the Flyers. He asked coach Floyd Smith to take him out of the nets after a bad first period. He believed in his heart that it would have been hopeless for him to stay in the game because he was not himself. Like a soldier manning a key outpost, Desjardins knew he was protecting, as well as working for, many others in his unit.

Desjardins was given relief and his team won the game but two nights later he forced himself back into the breach, despite his personal fears and doubts about his adequacy in the nets. This time he went out and did the job. With his men just barely protecting a one goal lead, Desjardins was threatened with a one-on-one breakaway as Ross Lonsberry of the Flyers skated in on a straight line from center ice toward the defenseless goalie. It was hockey's classic cobra against the mongoose confrontation.

Lonsberry faked to the left and faked to the right. Desjardins, his eyes riveted to the puck, slid out to blunt the attack. Lonsberry shot and the puck struck the outside of the metal post and glanced

*Islander goalie Glenn Resch was saved by a
lucky ricochet off a goalpost at a crucial moment, but at other times his skillful playing has
prevented many an enemy score.*

harmlessly away. The save won the game for Desjardins and his team. "You don't *think*," he says, "you rely on instinct."

With all deference to football linesmen, baseball catchers and the men who ride polo ponies, hockey players are *the* most courageous people in sports. They are able to withstand excruciating pain and seemingly insurmountable obstacles in their determination to stay on the ice and continue to play.

The examples are as numerous as sticks and pucks. Bobby Baun, a Toronto Maple Leafs' defenseman, once scored a Stanley Cup winning goal skating with a broken leg.

One night Dickie Moore of the Montreal Canadiens and Marcel Pronovost of the Detroit Red Wings skated at each other like a pair of heavy tanks. "We ran together," Moore recalls, "and I was determined to keep going. He was challenging me and I was challenging him. I got crunched into the boards and my wrist was broke. It was a fair check—just one of those things."

Moore's broken wrist was placed in a cast. A night later he returned to the Canadiens' lineup. It was midseason. He played every game on the schedule with his hand in a cast and, still, Dickie Moore won the scoring championship.

Nor are such heroic acts limited to the hardy old days. More recently, young Denis Potvin, New York Islanders' defenseman, played a hefty portion of the 1973–74 season with a broken foot. Potvin's teammate Garry Howatt led his team in fighting that same season although he was the Islanders' smallest player and is an epileptic to boot. Buffalo Sabres' sharpshooter Rick Martin wore a protective cast on his hand during the 1975 Stanley Cup play-offs.

Why do hockey players display such exceptional courage? Perhaps it is related to their Canadian heritage (more than 95 per cent of the big leaguers were originally Canadian) in which the rugged environment breeds rugged individuals. Consider some of the following examples:

In 1904 a team from Dawson City in the Klondike mining region of Canada's Yukon Territory were challengers for the Stanley Cup. The challenge itself wasn't so remarkable, except that Dawson City's opponent happened to be several thousand

miles away, in Ottawa, Ontario. That meant the Dawson City team had to cross a continent, partly on dogsled, to play their opponents.

The Klondike club left Dawson City on December 19, 1904, some of them running behind the dog teams, waving to gay crowds lining the route. The trip, which today can be made in eight hours of actual traveling time, took the Yukon players twenty-three days. As luck would have it, they missed the boat by two hours at Skagway, Alaska, and waited five days for the next one. Eventually they boarded a scow, the S.S. *Dolphin,* which finally arrived in Seattle. They then clambered aboard a train for Vancouver and finally another train for Ottawa. It would be romantic to report that they won the Stanley Cup after all that, but Ottawa won the two game total goal series.

An equally valorous journey involved Boston Bruins' defenseman Eddie Shore who missed his team's train for Montreal on January 2, 1929. The best defenseman of his era, Shore believed that nothing could be more catastrophic or embarrassing to him than missing a game.

Borje Salming is an example of the new breed of European skater who has adapted splendidly to the more rugged NHL style. A former member of the Swedish National Team, Salming was signed by the Toronto Maple Leafs in 1973 and became a league All-Star a season later.

Marcel Dionne, one of the most agile skaters in the NHL, and one of its most controversial, signed with the Los Angeles Kings in 1975 after several difficult years—and some pleasant moments too—with the Detroit Red Wings. The French Canadian ace won the Lady Byng Trophy for good sportsmanship and superior play in 1975.

What to do? It was 9 P.M. and the next train to Montreal was late on the following day. After several desperate phone calls, Shore reached a wealthy friend who offered him his limousine and chauffeur for the overnight expedition.

By then, a sleet storm was blasting Boston and beginning to take on all the aspects of a major blizzard, but Shore was unimpressed. The chauffeur called for him at 11:30 P.M. and the two began the 350-mile Boston–Montreal drive over ramshackle roads that meandered around and over New England mountains.

Shore asked the driver to speed up. "The man apologized," Shore said, "and told me he didn't have chains and, furthermore, didn't like driving in the winter. The poor fellow urged me to turn back to Boston."

No way. Shore bought tire chains, told the chauffeur to move over and decided to drive himself as the blizzard approached full force. Snow caked on either side of the line windshield wiper which eventually froze to the glass. Unable to see

out the window Shore removed the top half of the windshield.

Exposed to the icy wind, Shore steered the limousine across the Massachusetts border and up into the New Hampshire mountains. Around five in the morning Shore noted that the tire chains had worn out. Luckily, a road construction camp was at a turn in the road. Shore awakened the watchman and obtained a new set of tire chains, then continued northward toward Canada. The road was icier than a hockey rink. The car skidded off the road four times, but each time Shore and his chauffeur managed to push it back on the highway.

Finally, Shore asked the chauffeur to relieve him while he napped. Within seconds the Bruins' defenseman dozed off into a deep sleep. Then suddenly, the chauffeur lost control and the big car plunged into a ditch. Still undaunted Shore hiked a mile to a farmhouse.

"I paid eight dollars for a team of horses, harnessed them and pulled the car out of the ditch. By this time we weren't far from Montreal and I thought we'd make it before game time," he said.

They did—at 5:30 P.M., to be precise. Bruin coach Art Ross was awed by the sight of his abominably snow-covered defenseman. "His eyes were bloodshot," Ross said, "his face frostbitten and windburned, his fingers bent and set like claws after gripping the wheel so long. He couldn't even walk straight."

Ross insisted that Shore not dress for the game that night against Montreal but Eddie would have none of that. He took the ice for Boston and played fifty-six minutes of the sixty-minute game, missing those four minutes because of a pair of two-minute penalties.

Was the trip worth it? Well, Boston won the match, 1–0, and the game's only goal was scored by Eddie Shore.

It was an extraordinarily courageous performance, but not unusual for practitioners of the sport.

Consider the case of Maurice "Rocket" Richard, hockey's answer to Babe Ruth. The Montreal Canadiens' right wing was renowned for his blazing shot, the way Ruth was famous for his "tape measure" home runs. One of Richard's finest hours occurred on April 8, 1952, in the final play-off of a Boston–Montreal series.

Derek Sanderson, former Bruin, now a Ranger, often controversial, was inured to the life of a hockey professional very early.

With the score tied, 1–1, in the second period, Richard knifed through the enemy defenses. One of the defenders, Leo Labine, charged Richard, whacking the Rocket in the head with his stick and in the stomach with his knee. Richard keeled over on his back and to many spectators it looked like the end. His face smeared with blood, the Rocket finally clambered to his feet and skated groggily off the ice and to the arena hospital, where a deep cut over his left eye was stitched.

Nevertheless, with the score tied, 1–1, in the third period, Richard returned to the ice. He then took a pass from defenseman Butch Bouchard, skirted the Boston defense and scored the winning goal. Sitting on the bench, teammate Elmer Lach leaned forward and fainted.

Richard, himself, never fainted. But when the Rocket's father, Onésime Richard, walked into the dressing room after the game and put his arm around his son's shoulder, the Rocket broke down and cried like a baby.

Richard's invulnerability to pain was not unusual, at least not for hockey players, past or present. Like many of his contemporaries in the National Hockey League, Derek Sanderson of the New York Rangers was toughened up for the professional fray at an early age. His father, Harold Sanderson, started the toughening-up process when Derek was an eight year old in Niagara Falls, Ontario. One day, the six ounce hard rubber slammed into Derek's head, opening a large, bloody wound. The kid skated to the sidelines, expecting first aid treatment and commiseration from his father.

"You're all right," snapped Derek's father. "Get out there. The blood will dry. Shake it off!"

An hour elapsed before Harold Sanderson took his son to the hospital where three stitches were required to close the wound. Before the week was up, Derek returned to the doctor to have the stitches removed.

"Let *me* have them," Harold Sanderson said.

"When we got home," Derek recalled, "he put them in a little plastic box. He saved every one of my first one hundred stitches and pretty soon I started to become proud of them. I'd come home after a tough game and say, 'Hi, Dad, eight more stitches!'"

Keith Magnuson, one of Sanderson's NHL antagonists, also was hardened as a youth by his father. Early in Keith's life, Joe Magnuson took his flame haired son in tow and taught him the rudiments of boxing and the rewards of hard work.

"If you work for something hard enough," Joe Magnuson said, "you'll always attain it, with God's help."

The advice paid off for Keith, who in time became the leader of the Chicago Black Hawks' defense and one of the toughest men in the game. "As long as you're on the ice," Keith said, "you've got to keep coming back whether you want to or not. Once you get intimidated in hockey you just don't stay around."

One of the most notorious intimidators was Ted Green, a Boston Bruins' defenseman who became captain of the New England Whalers and then went on to the Jets in 1975. Green's comeback is one of the most remarkable in all sports. In September 1969 during an exhibition game, he sustained a fractured skull and was close to death. Following delicate surgery a plate was inserted in his head. Although Green missed the rest of the 1969–70 season, he eventually returned and was instrumental in helping Boston to a Stanley Cup victory in 1972.

The possibility of permanent injury, if not death, always threatens professional hockey players. During the 1974 play-offs, Philadelphia Flyers' defenseman Barry Ashbee lost the sight of an eye after being struck by a puck. But that didn't dim his enthusiasm for the game; he returned to the Flyers as an assistant coach.

Ashbee's teammate Bobby Clarke has emerged as one of the most courageous players of all. A diabetic, Clarke showed up at the Flyers' camp in September 1969 and passed out twice because of his condition. For a few days, there was a big question as to whether the strain and grind of big league play might just be too much for the rookie. But Clarke recovered, overcame his physical problems and developed into one of hockey's greatest stars. In both 1973 and 1975 he was named the Most Valuable Player in the NHL. And in 1974 and 1975 he captained Philadelphia to Stanley Cup victories.

Thus, courage, of which the skaters with sticks have more than a fair share, is another vital ingredient for participants in the war game called hockey.

So just as war is hell, so is hockey.

But—this is hockey!

A goalie's life is dangerous. For protection he wears upwards of 35 pounds of covering including heavy pads, well lined pants, a chest protector, a mask, two mitts and, of course, carries the heavy goalie stick.

Goaltending-
Deadly and
Demanding

It has been said, with some justification, that goaltending is the most demanding position in the realm of sport. The puck, a six ounce hunk of vulcanized rubber, is a terribly destructive missile, especially when it zooms from the stick of men such as Bobby Hull or Rick Martin or Guy Lafleur at speeds up to 140 miles per hour.

A man who attempts to block such missiles invites serious injury with the possibility of becoming permanently maimed. The tension induced by this fact can become unbearable. While there is no specific evidence that any goaltender has ever committed suicide, there is abundant proof that some goalies have frequently approached the breaking point.

More than four years after his retirement in 1971 National Hockey League goaltender Glenn Hall still displayed levels of worry lines engraved on his brow. Scar tissue around his mouth was a permanent souvenir of 75 stitches. Remnants of another 150 stitches decorated other parts of his face.

"Some guys," says Hall, "used their heads to stop the puck. I got my head out of the way—when I could. It didn't matter that the puck went into the net."

Preparing for a night of puck stopping turns the strongest stomach. In much the way bomber pilots would anguish before their runs over Germany in World War II, Hall would get the heaves before a game. "It was really a waste to feed him that day," his wife Pauline recalls.

Actually, Hall was more fortunate than the original goaltenders who took their positions in front of the goal line (there were no pipes then) in the 19th century when hockey was born.

In the early days the game was primitive in the extreme. Goaltenders wore no pads, and for a short time they survived without the need of gauze, iodine and adhesive tape. Today's skates with boots and blades riveted together were unheard of; instead players clamped blades to their street shoes by means of an unusual spring device that might or might not hold. This proved irksome to the goaltenders because when they stopped the puck with their skates, the impact invariably released the spring and propelled the blade to another section of the rink, thus requiring long stoppages of play to retrieve scattered skates.

The impact of puck against unprotected skin had the same effect on goaltenders that machine guns had against sabre-armed cavalry. There was panic, a disorderly retreat and, finally, some deep thinking to produce an antidote to goalie slaughter.

"Goalies had to figure out a way to save their legs from utter destruction," said Captain Sutherland, an early player with the Kingston (Ontario) Athletics. "What they did was simply figure out what their compatriots in cricket had done. They appropriated the wicketkeepers' leg pads and eventually progressed up the line to chest protectors and other safeguards."

23

Shero and faced Quaker City fans who weren't that sure about welcoming him back.

The decisive moment occurred on opening night against the Toronto Maple Leafs at Philadelphia's Spectrum. During the time Parent had played for Toronto, he had openly criticized the city. The Maple Leafs hungered for revenge.

However, they didn't get much satisfaction. The Flyers scored twice and Parent shut out the Leafs.

As the season progressed Parent improved. He compiled a record of 12 shutouts, three shy of the league record, and displayed the dexterity of his goaltending master, Jacques Plante.

Bernie's biggest smile was reserved for that moment on May 19, 1974, when the final buzzer sounded at the Spectrum and the Flyers had beaten Boston four games to two for the Cup.

Bernie and Flyers' captain Bobby Clarke cradled the ancient silver mug in their arms during the traditional post-game rites.

"Winning the Cup is not like I thought it would be," Parent said. "It is better than I thought it would be. It's a feeling you can't describe. I'll never forget this feeling; it will always be with me. So many guys play hockey and never win the Cup. I feel sorry for anyone who never experiences what I'm feeling."

By 1975 Parent had become an international celebrity and his masked visage appeared on the cover of *Time* in February of that year.

The terrific feeling experienced by Parent is shared by Philadelphians who summed up their reaction to their favorite goalie by buying thousands of bumper stickers printed with the apt comment ONLY THE LORD SAVES MORE THAN BERNIE PARENT!

In 1975 Parent and Philadelphians were able to experience that great feeling again as the Flyers won the Stanley Cup for the second year in a row.

The Biggest Goalie

It has been said that Gary Smith's goaltending style is a composite of "standard butterfly and panic." The butterfly is when Smith falls to his knees, sliding his legs out in both directions like a pair of butterfly wings. The panic comes any time he sees the hunk of rubber flak on an enemy's stick.

"I'm afraid of that puck," says Smith. "I respect the fact that every time it hits you it hurts."

At six-feet-four Smith is the tallest goalkeeper in professional hockey. He is also one of the most candid. He admits that the netminding business nearly drove him looney when he played for the Oakland Seals and faced nearly 70 shots a game. He says he'd get dizzy and be about to faint.

Gary, the son of former Bruins' star Des Smith, simply was suffering the normal goaltenders' affliction, "rubberitis." Goalies who see too many pucks coming at them often get dizzy and are close to fainting. In that sense Smith was quite normal.

Unlike many of the better NHL goaltenders, Smith was mired in a quicksand of team mediocrity and bad luck. He skated for poor performance teams in Oakland and in his first year in Vancouver; and when he played for Chicago Gary was understudy for Tony Esposito with whom he shared Vezina Trophy honors in 1971–72. But in the 1974–75 season with Vancouver things took a turn for the better. The Canucks developed smartly under manager-coach Phil Maloney and they finished first in their division.

Smith played in the 1975 NHL All-Star game, in which he was second only to Bernie Parent in the polling for best goalie. He was named the Canucks' most valuable player, most valuable teammate as well as most popular player.

Although he is in his thirties, Smith has not as yet settled upon a permanent playing style. His two years in Chicago working alongside Esposito encouraged Gary to use the butterfly (also known as the inverted V) stance but a near disaster during the 1974–75 season inspired Smith to switch to more of a stand-up position. During a game against the Buffalo Sabres, Jerry Korab, the huge Sabres' skater, broke through the Vancouver defenses for a shot at Gary.

Smith dropped to his knees, flaring his pads in the hopes that Korab would shoot low and to a corner. "Unfortunately," Gary recalls, "he shot it right at my head."

Although he was wearing a fiberglass protective mask, Smith sustained a broken cheekbone.

40

Right: *During the 1970's, Bernie Parent emerged as the premier goaltender of the NHL. While many factors go into a teams' success, ultimately it is the goaltender who blunts the enemy's final attack.*

Masked
Men

Few of today's goaltenders are able to do a perfect split, but Gary Inness of the 1974-75 Pittsburgh Penguins covers considerable ice with a well balanced block. His defenseman Dennis Owchar clears the neighborhood so that Inness can be prepared to snare the rebound.

Above: When a goalie is hot even the best shooters find it impossible to score. Glenn Resch of the New York Islanders was just such a hot goaltender during the 1975 Stanley Cup play-offs. Here he is stopping Philadelphia Flyers sharp shooter Bobby Clarke (left) Rick MacLeish (center) and Reg Leach (right) as the dark shirted Islanders come to the rescue.

Top Far Left: *Buffalo Sabres goalie Roger Crozier has mastered the art of springing from a fallen position to the normal goalie stance by using his right hand to grasp the crossbar of the net.*

Top Near Left: *An effective goaltending technique is "stacking" the pads. One goalie pad is placed on top of the other to cover a large segment of the net. Vancouver Canucks' goalie Gary Smith blocks a shot utilizing this method to perfection.*

Bottom Far Left: *Goalies frequently are called upon to leave their net area to intercept loose pucks that have eluded their defensemen. Rogatien Vachon of the Los Angeles Kings sprints from his cage to outrace the foe to the rubber.*

Bottom Near Left: *The kick save requires exquisite split second timing. One of the better exponents of the spread eagle is Dan Bouchard of the Atlanta Flames who watches the flying puck following his kick.*

Right: *All signals are go for Montreal Canadiens' goalie Ken Dryden. His trappers mitt is open, his stick is flat on the ice and he is standing up ready to make a perfect glove save.*

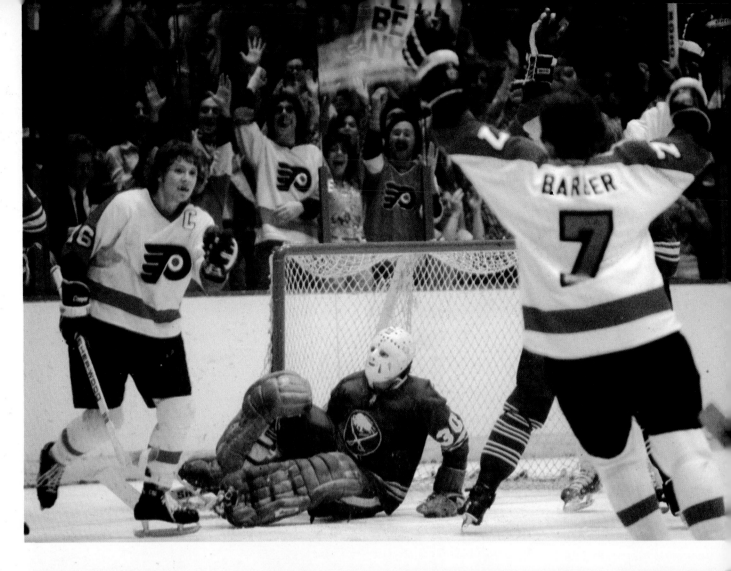

Top Right: A teammate can be a goalie's worst enemy if he "screens" his netminder. Cleveland Crusaders' goalie Gerry Cheevers just barely looks over the shoulders of a near-screening defenseman during WHA action.

Bottom Right: Some goalies have resorted to dancing lessons to sharpen their agility. Boston Bruins' goalie Gilles Gilbert appears to be demonstrating a dance step as he punts away a Rangers' shot.

Upper Left: A goaltender frequently is helpless when he leaves his skates. Buffalo Sabres' netminder Gerry Desjardins falls to the ice and remains immobilized as the Philadelphia Flyers' Bill Barber (7) scores during 1975 Stanley Cup title play. Flyer captain Bobby Clarke (left) is on hand to cheer.

Bottom Left: Soviet goalie Vladislav Tretiak does what a goaltender is supposed to do. He fills a lot of the net. He holds on to the upright with his hand to get the feel of the cage and rivets his eyes on the play in front of him, keeping his goal stick flat on the ice to blunt low shots. Team Canada left wing Bobby Hull waits impatiently for the pass that never comes.

Smith discarded the Esposito V and became more of a traditional, upright goalkeeper, whenever possible. However, he did retain other Esposito techniques. "I learned concentration from Tony," Gary says, "how to discipline myself when I'm on the ice. Tony told me he tries to keep the puck out for the first five minutes. He plays in five minute cycles. Now I do the same. Each five minutes I tell myself, there's no way they're going to score on me."

Nothing in Smith's early days suggested the concentration and fortitude that allowed him to play 72 out of 80 regular season games for the Canucks in 1974–75, the most for any NHL goaltender. His father Desmond, an NHL player for five years, had skated for the Stanley Cup winning 1941 Bruins but Gary was not especially gifted at any position. He dabbled at the forward positions in his native Ottawa and occasionally went between the pipes. One day his Little League baseball coach suggested that Gary play some hockey with a local team that needed a goalie.

One night during a game in Toronto, Smith was discovered by a Maple Leafs' scout. He was offered a scholarship to St. Michael's College (high school) as a goalie.

He succeeded Gerry Cheevers in the St. Mike's net and played well enough to become a pro at age 20. Since the Leafs were well goaled by Johnny Bower he was designated as an emergency replacement for whichever farm club needed help. Hence, his nickname, "Suitcase Smith." As he says, "I was sent wherever anybody got hurt—Rochester, Tulsa, Victoria."

In retrospect he finds it difficult to believe that he played the first three of his professional years barefaced in front of the oncoming pucks. His injuries have been many. The Korab shot will not likely be forgotten until long after he retires, nor will his broken ankle, fractured skull and strained groin. Each injury provided a lesson and helped remold the Smith style.

His colorful antics sometimes overshadow the fact that Gary Smith of the Vancouver Canucks has honed his skills to such an extent that he now is one of the most respected goalies in the NHL.

Top Left: The goaltender must be able to use his stick much in the manner of a defenseman or a forward. Tony Esposito of the Chicago Black Hawks poke checks the puck away from his goal crease so that an oncoming teammate can retrieve it.

Bottom Left: A game of inches: New York Rangers' goalie Gilles Villemure extends himself to the utmost making a spread-eagle save in which he spears the rubber with his outstretched right trapper's mitt. All goalies wear two separate and distinctly different gloves. The trapper's mitt resembles a first baseman's glove and it has ample room with which to field flying and rolling pucks. The outside of the other glove which is larger and heavily padded is used to deflect flying discs while the inside is used for grasping the goal stick.

Because of his exceptional size (six-feet-four), goalie Gary Smith of the Vancouver Canucks fills more of the net than most. This makes it more difficult for shooters such as Greg Polis of the Rangers to find open spaces through which to drill the puck.

Tall goaltenders like Smith and Montreal's Ken Dryden are considered less agile than more miniscule types such as Gilles Villemure, Rogatien Vachon and Glenn Resch. The lanky goalies compensate for their lack of agility by outthinking the enemy.

Smith has a casual approach to life, but this is deceptive. Sure, he worries about getting killed by a flying puck and realizes his NHL years are numbered no matter how lucky he is. Yet, he does silly things that have caused sportswriters to label him a "flake." He resents the designation because his so-called flakiness is really a safety valve for the pressure cooker life of a goaltender.

One of Smith's japes is called the torn-dollar-bill-trick. He tears a dollar bill in half and puts one piece in a ticket envelope and drops it in a prominent place. He likes to watch the reactions of people who pick it up. Another safety valve pastime is

placekicking shoes over signs as he waits in airline terminals.

Smith tries to avoid practice sessions in which more than 200 shots are fired at each goaltender. Such an attitude is not unique. The best goalies such as Lorne Worsley and Glenn Hall always loathed practice. Like Hall, Smith hates the pregame tension that grips him beginning on the morning of a game. He says that the games themselves are relatively easy, but that he is scared all day and that the worst part is waiting.

While Bernie Parent's diversions are hunting and fishing, Smith's avocation is horse racing. He owns a trotter named Don's Bow and unabashedly admits that he would go anywhere to see a horse race. Gerry Cheevers also feels the same way. Gary also enjoys skiing even though the Canucks, technically, forbid any player to ski for fear of potential injury. He doesn't care. He figures the relaxation is more important than the silly team rules. "If I break a leg up there I'll wait until the next morning, get to the rink somehow, and fall down on the ice and break it."

Suitcase Smith respects life, fears his job and will—for the duration—live it up until he gets his walking papers. Someday he may yet win the Vezina Trophy all by himself and if he does the chances are that Gary Smith will just keep on being Gary Smith telling the world, "I'm not a superstar."

Hockey's Renaissance Man

He reminds intellectuals of a young John Kenneth Galbraith. He is tall, articulate and commanding, both physically and. intellectually. He is an attorney. He can discuss complex social and political subjects such as consumerism and American foreign policy with consummate ease and sure knowledge. As an activist he has worked with Ralph Nader investigating the problems of commercial fishermen.

Goaltenders must be in superb physical condition once the season begins because their work is the most taxing and body contorting of any of the players. Faked out of position, Montreal Canadiens' goalie Ken Dryden clumsily stabs out with his left trapper's glove in an attempt to blunt an enemy shot.

Ken Dryden is many things to many people but mostly he is renowned as the Montreal Canadiens' crack goaltender; a *Renaissance* man who once walked out of the National Hockey League limelight and a $100,000 a year salary in favor of a $7,000 a year job as a law clerk. "Hockey," he says, "is just one of the things I do. And I do a number of things. I'm interested in hockey when I am playing hockey but that certainly is not my whole life."

There have been intellectuals who have starred in big league hockey in the past but they have been few. None have been as fascinating as Ken Dryden.

The Dryden saga began in the Toronto suburb of Islington, Ontario. His father, Murray, built goals from two-by-fours and chicken wire and placed them in the driveway so the boys in the neighborhood could play ball hockey. "I played one goal and my brother Dave, who is now a WHA goalie, played the other," says Ken. "That's all there was to it. We had tournaments every Saturday. Rubber balls were crummy on the pavement, but tennis balls were great. They stung more, too."

His parents insisted that he hit the books as often as he handled the puck. Even in his pre-teen years Ken displayed the ability to combine successfully the cerebral and the physical. He was a seven-year-old rookie with the Humber Valley Atoms. At eight, he goaled for the Humber Valley Pee-wees, although two to three years younger than his teammates.

By age 15 he had "pro" written all over him and the Canadiens zeroed in with an offer. They wanted him to play Junior A hockey—the fastest amateur league—in Peterborough, Ontario. Ken was planning to enter Grade 13, the most important Canadian academic year, and there would be a lot of pressure on him to do well in the classroom. He couldn't see how playing hockey and trying to go to school in Peterborough would work, so he stayed in Toronto.

Eventually, Dryden went to Cornell University, received a $200 annual honorary scholarship and, in time, playing on the Cornell team, became an All-American goaltender. He was then accepted as a student at Harvard Law School.

But Harvard would not allow Ken to play hockey. He rejected Cambridge and accepted an offer from the Canadian National Team, a newly formed group organized to play in international competi-

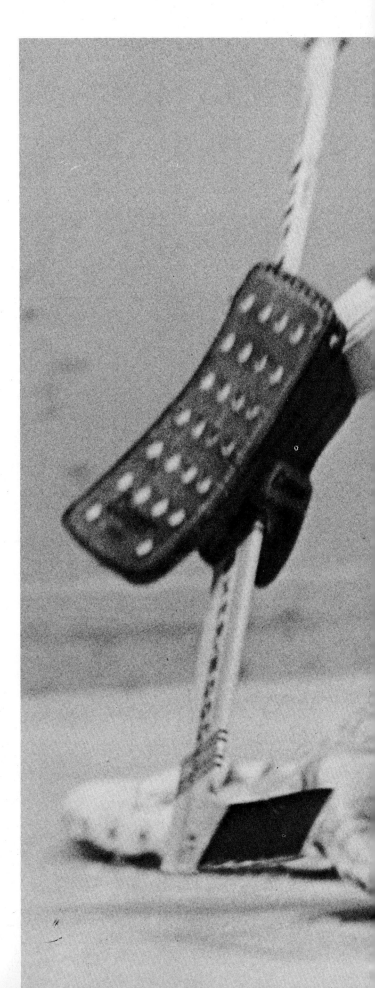

Goaltenders, like forwards and defensemen, are finicky about their equipment. Goalie Ken Dryden of the Canadiens has experimented with various face masks. This is one he later abandoned for a more extensive head and face covering.

After obtaining a law degree, Canadien's goalie Ken Dryden returned to his team for the 1974-75 season. The Buffalo Sabres proved to be more taxing than legal problems for Ken in the 1975 Stanley Cup semifinals. The puck can be seen threading its way between Dryden's open legs.

tion, which included full tuition at the law school of the University of Manitoba in Winnipeg.

When the National Team folded a year after Ken had signed, Canadiens' manager Sammy Pollock rushed in with an offer which would allow Dryden to play pro hockey while he attended McGill University Law School in Montreal. Dryden accepted and became a weekend goaltender for the American Hockey League's Montreal Voyageurs.

Everything about his style suggested a long and gratifying future in the NHL. He was cool, sure and able but his intellectual ability frightened the anti-intellectual hockey crowd, which annoyed Dryden.

Dryden made his NHL debut in the spring of 1971 when he played a few insignificant late season games for the Canadiens. Then, unexpectedly, he was designated as starting goalie against the then mighty Boston Bruins in the Stanley Cup finals. He blunted the best of Bobby Orr's shots, foiled Phil Esposito and carried the Canadiens to the Cup in one of big time sport's major upsets. His credentials for major league status were definitely established.

Within two years Dryden had won the Vezina Trophy and the Canadiens another Stanley Cup. There he was sitting on top of the hockey world when he walked away from the game prior to the opening of training camp in 1973. He took a job "articling" for the Toronto law firm of Osler, Hoskin and Harcourt. Canadiens' manager Sammy Pollock had asked Dryden to play for less than Ken thought he was worth. Ken decided to sit it out as his move sent shock waves through the NHL.

"I would not have thought of articling if the problem with the Canadiens didn't exist," Dryden explained. "But, in retrospect, the year off was the best thing for me. I probably would have played hockey until I was 35 and then gone back and taken the bar exam. I would have been ten years out of touch."

So at the age of 26 he went into temporary retirement, a somewhat unique experience in professional sports.

His love of hockey remained. In his spare time he played defense for a local industrial league team and did color commentary for television broadcasts of WHA games. But he missed the Canadiens and they missed him. The result was a rapproche-

ment during the summer of 1974 and a new NHL contract for Ken.

Dryden's return was no simple matter. His impetuous exit in 1973 had antagonized teammates and emphasized the gulf between Dryden the intellectual and the more familiar, less articulate hockey player.

Two major obstacles, one emotional, the other physical, were present. Had Dryden been a forward or a defenseman, he would have been less conspicuous and, therefore, less vulnerable to the effects of the limelight. Then, there was the matter of his reflexes. Had the year away from the NHL firepower dulled his ability to block shots?

In the early weeks of the 1974–75 season it appeared that the answer to the last question was in the affirmative. Yes, Dryden was a flop. A big flop. In a game against Los Angeles at the Montreal Forum the $175,000 a year Canadiens' goalie played so horrendously that the partisan fans showered him with boos.

What had happened to this once impregnable goaltender? Was this anxious fellow the one who once had won the Conn Smythe Trophy, the Calder and Vezina prizes? Had he lost all confidence?

The layoff accentuated problems unique to goaltending such as timing. Timing is the difference between having the puck bounce off the heel of the glove or catching it in the pocket.

Dryden explained some of his other problems, "There was the concentration, disciplining myself to concentrating for the complete 60 minutes. Then, there's the backdrop of confidence a goalie must have. When you're playing well, you acquire confidence in your ability, which is one of a goalie's most important assets. You only build it up through a series of good performances."

Confidence didn't return quickly for Dryden. He played badly in October and November of 1974. During a span of five games he allowed 22 goals; critics openly wondered whether the once king of the goaltenders was all washed up at the age of 27. Ken, himself, wondered and was disheartened and discouraged.

The Canadiens carried two backup goalies, Bunny Larocque and Wayne Thomas. Larocque got the nod as Dryden's replacement while Ken sat on the bench and studied his teammate.

Dryden's problems were magnified by the Canadiens' inability to solidify a hold on first place. A surprising Los Angeles Kings' team raced neck and neck with the Canadiens for the lead as the season approached the homestretch in February 1975. Just when it appeared that Larocque had captured the number one goaltending job, he faltered and Dryden once again got the call.

He returned more analytical of his goaltending than ever. There is, according to Dryden, a similarity between defensive hockey and defensive football. "In football," Dryden explains, "the best team may not be the best defensively. They don't have to be the first against the rush and first against the pass. They may be third or fourth. But the *defense only bends. It never breaks.* There are no longer gainers—no bombs.

"Hockey is much the same. We have to be disciplined enough that at times although we may give up the puck or we may get into some difficulty, we should never leave a man alone with the puck in front of the net. We should never allow breakaways. Those are high percentage shots. A lot of goals are going to be scored on shots like that. That's hockey's version of the bomb and that's what has to be stopped."

As if touched by a magic wand, Dryden became the super-goalie of other years. Dancing in the Canadiens' goal, wearing his preposterous medieval equipment, he goaled Montreal past Los Angeles and firmly into a first place finish. At least two million Montrealers breathed easier once more.

An Instinctive Goalie

If Ken Dryden is the thinking man's goaltender, Gerry Cheevers is the instinctive man's goalie.

Says Cheevers, "I play goal mostly by reflex and intuition, making the move that seems most appropriate at the time. Routine saves are routine; exceptional saves are instinct and experience."

Cheevers' instinct and experience first achieved international acclaim when he played for the Boston Bruins and they won the Stanley Cup in 1970. Behind Bobby Orr and Phil Esposito was this lighthearted goaltender who provided the necessary defensive strength for an assault minded hockey club. Suddenly, goalies from Detroit to Des Moines were taking a careful look at the Cheevers style.

"My best asset," Cheevers has said, "is my ability to skate. I'm extremely agile and agility is the key to skating. Also, I figure I'm a good play-off goaltender—maybe because I'm a good competitor. When all is said and done, though, skating is what made me a good goaltender. I believe skating is the greatest asset a goaltender can have."

Gerry's father was coach of the Catholic Youth Organization team in St. Catherines, Ontario, and started Gerry out as a forward at the age of seven. He developed his skating technique and might have become a big league scorer were it not for an unexpected development. His father put him in the goalie position when the regular young goalie didn't show up and he stayed there.

Gerry learned fast and eventually won an audition with the Toronto Maple Leafs. He made it but

The mask enclosed goalie frequently looks like a spaceman with his grotesque helmet covering head and face. It's refreshing to see a maskless goalie every so often. Ken Dryden of the Montreal Canadiens sheds his mask during a respite in the action.

was destined to skate in the shadow of Toronto ace Johnny Bower. His transfer to the Bruins was a blessing to Cheevers and the Bruins. The goalie and the team matured together. At first Gerry regarded his abilities lightly. He called himself "a fat Peggy Fleming" and told the world that Glenn Hall, Tony Esposito and Eddie Giacomin were the best goalies in the world.

"At the time," says Cheevers, "Hall was *the* goaler. He did it all although I always felt his style would hurt his durability. I was a discord of leaps and flops, working from a crouch. When Tony Esposito came along he was as unorthodox as Hall. Tony's a righthanded shot, which means he catches the

puck with his right hand, the reverse of most goaltenders and giving him a turned-around look to the shooters. Tony is a competitor. He challenges the puck. He's quick, big and strong. He has all the assets. The thing that makes Giacomin so good is his skating. I'm convinced that if a goaltender ever scores a goal it's going to be Giacomin or Gary Smith or me."

Cheevers was at the peak of his career when the Bruins won the Stanley Cup again in 1972. It was then that he opted for the new World Hockey Association and signed a lucrative multi-year contract with the fledgling Cleveland Crusaders. It was felt that Cheevers was capable of carrying the new expansion team on his goal stick and, in a sense, he did.

Gerry was as daring and as spectacular as he had been with the Bruins. In September 1974 he was named the starting goaltender for Team Canada II in the eight game series against the Soviet National Team.

Once a Bruin, Gerry Cheevers, who later joined the WHA's Cleveland Crusaders, is an outspoken advocate of the protective face mask. Each set of stitches on Cheevers' mask represents an injury he would have suffered had his face been left unprotected.

The Art of Goaltending

The last line of defense against an enemy determined to score a goal is the goaltender who must, by the very nature of his position, employ many flexible shot blocking techniques to cope with the plethora of pucks that come his way from many directions and at many levels.

In the end, all that really matters is the goalie's ability to put body, stick, glove or other equipment in front of the puck and prevent it from going into the net.

A goalkeeper's equipment includes heavy pads for his legs and chest, a trapper's mitt for one hand to grab the puck and a large, heavily padded, protective glove for the other hand which also holds the goalie's stick. The blade of the goalie's stick has a maximum width of 3½ inches and widens to 4½ inches where the blade joins the shaft. A broadened section 3½ inches wide extends part way up the shaft. Depending on the height of the goalie the length of his stick will vary as long as it does not exceed 55 inches. Practically every goaltender wears a mask these days.

The standard—or classical—method of goaltending requires that the netminder remain on his feet when confronted by a shot. This technique is based upon the fact that a shot on goal often produces rebounds and a goaltender who loses his feet making the first save is vulnerable to the potential shot following the rebound while he is horizontal.

Bernie Parent of the Philadelphia Flyers, certainly one of the best goalies of the 1970s, adheres to the stand-up style more than most. But like his colleagues, Parent has been compelled by the nature of high-speed hockey to alter the technique to suit specific situations.

Therefore, if Parent is forced to make a stand-up save, he might find himself in a situation which calls for him to do something other than remain on his feet. A goaltender's repertoire includes a number of other standard responses. *Stacking The Pads:* One of the most effective methods. The goaltender slides to his left or right, depending upon the direction from which the shot is coming, and stacks one of his

Chicago Black Hawks' goalie Tony Esposito uses his mitt with the heavy outer padding to deflect the puck away from the net to the corner.

When the stick and the pads fail a goaltender he often can rely on his trapper's mitt, not unlike a first baseman's mitt. Goalie Phil Myre of the Atlanta Flames manages to thrust his mitt in front of a high flying puck just before it reaches the goal.

huge leather goalie pads upon the other. This double wall of pads covers a considerable amount of "air," or space into which a shooter might fire the puck.

The pads might be stacked when a goaltender guarding one side of the net is confronted by a sudden pass to the opposite side. Under most circumstances, he would be unable to cover the open side by maintaining a stand-up position. However, the slide and stack move is one of the quickest ways of getting from one side of the goal crease to the other. Hence, its frequent use.

The Spread-Eagle: Another method often used to block a distant portion of the net is the spread-eagle or split save. This blocking technique begins with the goalie in the upright position. If the puck appears to be heading for either side of the cage, the goalie thrusts his left (or right) skate along the ice toward the far corner of the net. This enables him to block the rubber with his skate blade, boot or pad as long as it is a low shot; if high, the puck will sail over the equipment. While the skate thrust toward one corner ostensibly is blocking the shot, the goalie's other skate and pad are flat on the ice, that skate often being wedged against the far goalpost for stability as well as coverage of the other corner. In executing the spread-eagle, the goalie hopes to cover the entire front of the six foot goalmouth.

A perfect split save is rare because of the difficulty of stretching one's legs wide enough to cover the entire net. More often the goalie will do a modified split, leaving air beneath his legs and some air at one of the ends of the cage.

In doing the split save—and sometimes in pad stacking—the goalie will try to keep his glove hand (the trapper's mitt) in a catching position. If he's doing a spread-eagle, the mitt will be extended to either the left or the right (depending upon his style), at the ready, to nab a flying shot. In the pad stacking position, his mitt arm would remain aloft, in the hopes of deflecting or catching a shot that might elude the pads.

Stopping Slap Shots: Since the advent of the slap shot, in which the speed of the puck increased up to 130 miles per hour, goaltenders have insisted that the puck is often almost impossible to see. To cope with this situation, goalies use a block that anticipates where the puck might go without actually being able to watch it.

Upon seeing a player winding up for a slap shot, the goalie drops to his knees (frequently spreading his legs in a V formation), keeping one hand in a catching position and the other free to deflect shots.

Screened Shots: Goaltenders have a healthy fear of the "screened" shot, one in which players block his view (or screen him from seeing the puck), until it is past him or hits his equipment. Some goalies try to keep a line on screened shots by looking over the other men's shoulders. Others prefer to drop to their knees in the hopes that they will see the rubber, and if not, hope then that their legs will cover enough net to block the shot. Still others crouch, looking between the legs of the skaters screening him.

Naturally, it is easier for a goaltender if he can see the puck. The longer the shot, the easier it would seem to see a drive heading for him. On occasion, however, a goaltender's vision will be partially obscured by his own protective mask. This may happen if the puck is at his feet or when a player carrying the puck comes from behind him, around one side to a position in front of the net. The mask inhibits the goalie's peripheral vision in situations like this.

Sometimes the goalkeeper will "flop" on the puck; sometimes he'll catch it in his trapper's mitt or deflect it with his large glove. He uses his stick to make a stick save or pass the rubber to a teammate.

Few coaches, managers or fans are particularly concerned about *how* the netminder stops the puck as long as he keeps the biscuit from going over the red goal line.

As play swirls about him, Rangers' goalie Gilles Villemure hugs the corner of his net, jamming his left skate against the goalpost as he maintains his line of vision to the puck ahead.

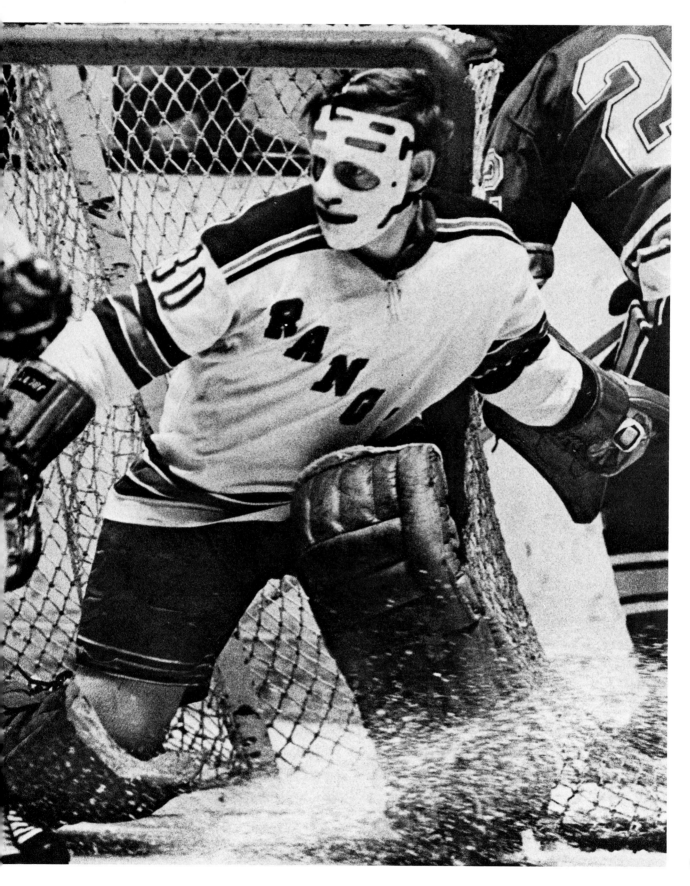

Hockey's "Roadrunner," Yvan Cournoyer of the Montreal Canadiens. Lightning fast from a standing start, Cournoyer specializes in out-racing enemy defensemen and then booming his heavy slap shot past opposition goaltenders. Compact (five-feet-seven and 165 lbs.), Cournoyer occasionally is intimidated by larger opponents.

Master Plans— Strategy of the Ice

Hockey strategy, in its most basic form, was vividly demonstrated one afternoon by Dick Irvin, when he was coaching a disoriented Chicago Black Hawks club in 1956. The grey haired Irvin ordered the team trainer and equipment-manager to carry one full-sized goal net off the ice and into the Chicago Stadium dressing room.

When the players trooped in for their pre-game chalk talk that afternoon, they were greeted by their coach leaning on the red cross bar with an official NHL puck in his palm. As soon as the final player had taken his seat, Irvin delivered the shortest and, in the opinion of many, the only hockey lesson, in the most vivid manner possible.

Drawing back his arm the coach threw the puck into the net, causing the twine to bulge. "And that, gentlemen," Irvin stated, "is what the game is all about!"

In a sense, Irvin was right, but it didn't help. The Black Hawks finished dead last in the league that season. Perhaps Irvin would have done better had he adopted a more involved strategy.

Overall strategy can be divided into two categories—offensive and defensive. In the mid-1940s the Toronto Maple Leafs won three consecutive Stanley Cups employing what was basically a defensive style. They would allow the more offense oriented clubs such as the Montreal Canadiens to pour into their zone. They would then contain the big guns and wait for a break that would enable them to move through an opening in the enemy armor.

Coached by Hap Day, the Leafs also put emphasis on clutch-and-grab hockey in which defensemen, and an occasional forward, would hamper the enemy by manacling an opponent's arm with a grab of the glove or a semi-embrace—hopefully out of sight of the referee. Variations on the Toronto clutch-and-grab system have survived through the seventies, especially as practiced by teams such as the Los Angeles Kings and Philadelphia Flyers.

The defensive approach frequently presupposes a weaker scoring team that could not stress heavy shooting even if it wanted to win via that route. Offense oriented clubs require big guns. The Montreal Canadiens had such weaponry in the fifties (Jean Beliveau, Maurice Richard, Boom Boom Geoffrion) and sixties (Yvan Cournoyer, Henri Richard, Phil Goyette) and they minimized defensive play. More recently the Buffalo Sabres have stressed speed skating and hard shooting over clutch and grab.

Tall, husky Peter Mahovlich has one of the longest reaches of any NHL forward. A sensitive skater, it has been said of Mahovlich that he reacts more to a pat on the rump than a thump on the earlobes.

Accenting "The French Connection" line, the Sabres prefer winning by outscoring the opposition rather than by outdefending them. With Gil Perreault, Rene Robert and Richard Martin, the Sabres possess some of the hardest shooters and fastest skaters hockey has known.

Somewhere in between the big offense and the heavy defense is the middle of the road strategy featured by a team like the New York Rangers which frequently has created a balance between hotshot scorers and capable defenders. Then, there are the unique strategies that revolve around special stars such as Bobby Orr and Phil Esposito of the Boston Bruins, a defenseman and a center, respectively, who concentrate on scoring with virtually no apparent concern for goals against.

Carrying out defensive plans against these two men can present a difficult problem for their opponents not just because of their great talents but also because of the positions they play. Center

Esposito ranges all over the ice. The opponents would like to use their normal leech-like operations against him, and dispute his territorial claims in the goal crease. But the presence of the ubiquitous defenseman Orr frequently distracts the foe from Esposito. Because he has been the most successful puck carrying defenseman, Orr has inspired a number of defensive brainstorms directed specifically against his speed and puck carrying talents.

The most emphatic anti-Orr maneuver was launched by the then St. Louis Blues' coach Scotty Bowman during the 1970 Stanley Cup finals between the Bruins and Blues. Until that time it had been unheard of for a defenseman to be shadowed (guarded) throughout his turn on the ice by an enemy checker. But Bowman broke tradition when he assigned Jimmy Roberts to regular duty as Orr's shadow. The one and only order given to Roberts was to attach himself to Orr, figuratively, no matter what transpired elsewhere on the ice.

"The guy did a good job," says Orr. "My shirt stayed dry and the way he stayed with me I could have had time for lunch. But when they play that way, it just leaves one of the other guys on our team open."

Which is precisely how Bowman's strategy backfired. Orr did not score a goal, nor did he register an assist in the game, but Johnny Bucyk scored a three goal hat trick and Boston triumphed, 6–1. Bowman got the message and discarded the permanent shadow plan.

"We knew the St. Louis team didn't have much of a chance in that series," says Bowman, "so there was an opportunity to try something new at no great expense. But nobody can really do that kind of job against Orr with his changes of speed."

More recently Bowman, as coach of the Montreal Canadiens, shifted his anti-Orr plans, instructing his left winger of the moment to be conscious of Orr all the time. One night, however, left wing

Steve Shutt watched in awe as Orr fooled him with bobs, weaves and power skating.

"I knew what I was supposed to do," says Shutt. "He just didn't give me time to do it."

Orr not only confounds the enemy with his multifaceted abilities but also generates unusual powers of leadership. This intangible factor can make or break a hockey club as the Canadiens discovered following the retirement of their distinguished captain Jean Beliveau and the aging of his successor, Henri Richard.

"The one thing we haven't developed," says goalie Ken Dryden of the Canadiens, "is an on the ice leader. We haven't had a mercurial player who can lift a team and turn a game around. But that is something that can happen overnight in a single play-off series. Philadelphia gets it from Bobby Clarke. Buffalo gets it from Gil Perreault. And Boston gets it from Bobby Orr and Phil Esposito. It's something you have to have."

Yet, the strategy centering on a single star can be just as damaging, if not more so, than the

Three brawny skaters pursue the rubber. Left to right: Jim Schoenfeld of the Sabres, Greg Polis of the Rangers and the Sabres' Jerry Korab.

65

blueprint involving team play at the expense of the individual.

A more recent battle plan has stressed physical play as much as scientific pattern passing and stickhandling. Philadelphia Flyers' coach Fred Shero is one who believes that an adjunct to natural talent is courage; and courage must be cultivated. He frequently will station one of his players in front of the net during practice and order a teammate to harass the player in any way possible, the idea being to enhance the skater's ability to take punishment.

"A typical hockey fan would probably tell you Frank Mahovlich is a great hockey player because he scored 49 goals in one year," Shero says. "But if I put Frank Mahovlich in a corner and send someone in to check him, he'll throw a blind pass into the slot every time, just to keep from getting hit.

"That kind of careless pass can send the other team away three-on-two if it's intercepted. The mark of a great player? Hardly. You won't see one of our players throw the puck away like that. It takes courage to take a hit in the corner, but our players will accept that to make a good pass."

Coaching strategy also includes the proper use of psychological warfare. Shero has continuously captured headlines using an unorthodox approach with newspapermen. In May 1975 when the Flyers were defending the Stanley Cup they had won a year earlier, Shero, expecting to face the Canadiens in the finals, stunned newsmen by declaring, "Most people, in particular the Canadian hockey fans, don't know *bleep* about hockey. They think they know what's good but they don't." Shero's outrageous oratory moved one Montreal columnist to reply, "Shero has declared war on all of Canada."

One of the most skillful shooters, Jim Pappin, formerly of the Chicago Black Hawks, tries to find an opening against New York Rangers' goalie Ed Giacomin. Pappin is attempting to skate around the goalie and shoot into an opening. However, the alert Giacomin is moving with the shooter, covering up as much area as possible along the way.

But his insightful opponent, Scotty Bowman, realized that this was just another sly but clever stratagem. "Shero will say anything if he thinks it will get his team going. When the Flyers played Toronto in the 1975 play-offs he needled Toronto hockey fans. He wanted to get the crowd riled up for his team. If you boo a good hockey player, you bring out the best in him."

Shero has specialized in criticizing his coaching colleagues for their inefficient use of strategy. He has expressed disapproval of the number of lines used by a team, of the way players are rotated between lines and of the number of players who don't dress for a game.

No individual pursues new strategic angles with the zeal of Fred Shero. In the summer of 1974 he went to Russia for a coaching clinic after the Flyers had won the Stanley Cup. "I'm still learning," he said. "At least I realize I don't know everything. Trouble is, most coaches don't know—and certainly won't admit—that they don't know everything about coaching."

Other coaches minimize the value of involved strategy, insisting that a few basics are really enough. "The word 'system'," says Los Angeles Kings' coach Bob Pulford, "is a grossly misused term. Our system is really not any different from what the other clubs use. The difference is, we make our system *work*. They have to believe in it. They have to be disciplined."

Then, there are factors that surmount strategies of all kinds. These are the psychological turns in a game or a series, the events that shift the momentum from one club to another. In the 1975 Stanley Cup quarterfinal between the New York Islanders and Pittsburgh Penguins, the Islanders won the series by winning four consecutive games after losing the first three straight. After the fourth game—the first won by the Islanders—the momentum switched to the Islanders. The Penguins were never able to regain the upbeat they had maintained in the opening three contests.

But there always seems to be an exception to these rules. That same spring, the Buffalo Sabres had won two games in a row from the Montreal Canadiens in the semifinals and also had momentum. Then, Montreal disrupted their advance by winning the next two matches. It appeared that the Canadiens had captured the momentum and would surely win the series. But it just doesn't always happen that way as Montreal goalie Ken Dryden learned.

"You can have a feeling of momentum immediately after a game like the second in a row that we had won," says Dryden. "But it lasts only until the first shift of the following game. If the other team comes out and plays it the way we want to, instead of the way they played in the previous game, they'll take it right away from you.

"And they did. The Sabres swarmed. They had all of us exhausted and running around."

Buffalo also won the next two games and the series. Momentum in hockey, like strategy, is where you find it.

Shot blocking by a forward or defenseman is one of hockey's most heroic maneuvers and also one of the most painful when the puck or a skate hits a player in an unprotected spot. Gerry O'Flaherty of the Vancouver Canucks learns this lesson the hard way.

Playing Techniques

To the uninitiated eye hockey is a formless game, a seemingly spontaneous and endless melange featuring a wildly bouncing puck, frenzied skaters and a baffled and beleaguered goaltender. Actually, hockey is, in many ways, a finely planned game replete with tactics and strategy ad infinitum.

Some of the more common offensive maneuvers include complex attacking formations like the power play and simple ploys such as the drop pass.

The power play is set in motion when the opposition is short a man because of a penalty. The basic aim of the power play is to score a goal while the opposition remains shorthanded. The essential ingredients of the power play include an expert playmaker, at least two hard shooters and a pair of rugged skaters to handle the heavy infighting that is expected to take place.

Ideally, the power play begins with a face-off deep in the enemy zone. The center, who takes the face-off, attempts to push the puck back to one of the two "point men" stationed at either the left or right side of the blue line. Normally, hard shooters, the point men, then attempt to find a free teammate closer to the goal and in scoring position. If the defense has the attackers well covered, the point man has the option either to take a shot on goal—most likely a booming slap shot—or to pass off laterally to his other point man who will attempt to again put the rubber in an advantageous shooting position. Power play styles vary from coach to coach, but the hoped for result is always the same—a flashing red goal light.

When teams are playing with the same number of men the number of available plays is endless. A common and highly effective gimmick is for a stickhandler to move into the enemy zone side by side with a line mate while the third member of the unit trails behind. If the teammate alongside is free a pass can be attempted. However, if he is covered the puck carrier will often drop the puck behind him for

With the puck at Stan Mikita's backhand (instead of his forehand), the Chicago center looks for a free teammate to whom to pass the puck. Then he will move into a more advantageous position from which to score.

The best scorers have their favorite places from which they can score. New York Rangers' left wing Steve Vickers favors a spot just to the left of the enemy goal from which to accept a pass and shoot. Don Lever (right) of the Vancouver Canucks attempts to keep Vickers out of the play with a push of his elbow and chest.

the forward who is following. By so doing the advance man can move toward the net, attempting to block the goalie's view while the shooter moves in and drills the puck at the net from behind the human screen.

A frequently executed play to relieve pressure on a defending team, and to launch a counterattack, begins when the defending team captures the puck in its own zone and it is passed to a teammate at the center red line. This is designed to catch the enemy defense flat-footed. If the long pass works the receiver will obtain the puck beyond the trapped opposition defense and be in position for a one-on-one thrust, otherwise known as a breakaway, against the lone goalie.

There have been those who claim that the science of carrying and manipulating the puck, otherwise known as stickhandling, is a lost art. Actually, the relative speed of hockey has increased so rapidly in the past 30 years that the techniques of stickhandling have been appropriately altered.

Normally, a player carrying the puck will have two hands on his stick, one at the top of the shaft and the other a quarter or halfway down. He will dribble the puck by manipulating it from one side of the stick blade to the other. Most major leaguers are able to dribble the puck at high speed without actually keeping their eyes on the rubber. They do it by "feel."

His eyes fixed on the defense ahead, Detroit forward Nick Libett skates through no-man's-land toward the enemy line. Spotting an opening, he prepares to cross his right leg over his left in order to maneuver around the edge of the opposition defensive unit.

71

When the puck carrier is challenged by an opponent, normally a defenseman, in a head to head confrontation stickhandling comes to the fore as the defender attempts to capture the puck. The stickhandler will either pass to a teammate, shoot the puck into the corner or on goal, or most intriguing of all, try to outwit the enemy with a strategic maneuver. This involves synchronized movements of the head, skates and stick. By bobbing his head back and forth the attacker attempts to confuse his foe. He then will try a run around either side of his opponent. The standard technique in such a stickhandling operation is called "the quick, wide, lateral dribble." The stickhandler pretends to "give" the puck to his opponent. When the opponent lunges for it the attacker pushes the puck wide of the defender in a lateral motion either to the left or right. He thus propels the puck, hopefully, out of the range of the defender's stick. He then skates around the trapped foe.

There are many variations on this operation, but basically it involves the ability to move around the opponent without permitting him to capture the puck.

Although some purists frown on it, another effective stickhandling device involves the use of only one hand, holding the stick at its very top, and cradling the puck with the stick blade far out from the body. In this way an attacker might attempt an end run around the right side of his opponent's defense. He would carry the puck far to his right, holding the stick in one hand while using his free left hand as a fender to intercept enemy sticks or bodies.

Stickhandling also is effective in one-on-one situations when a shooter skates alone against a goaltender. The shooter has the opportunity either to fire the puck at the net or to try to lure the goalie out of position by stickhandling. In this cat and mouse situation the stickhandler will attempt to force the goalie to leave his skates and fall to the ice. He will do this by maneuvering the puck back and forth to a point where the netminder believes he has an opportunity to smother the rubber. At this juncture the wide stickhandler will pull the puck back from the goalie's grasp and attempt to move it lat-

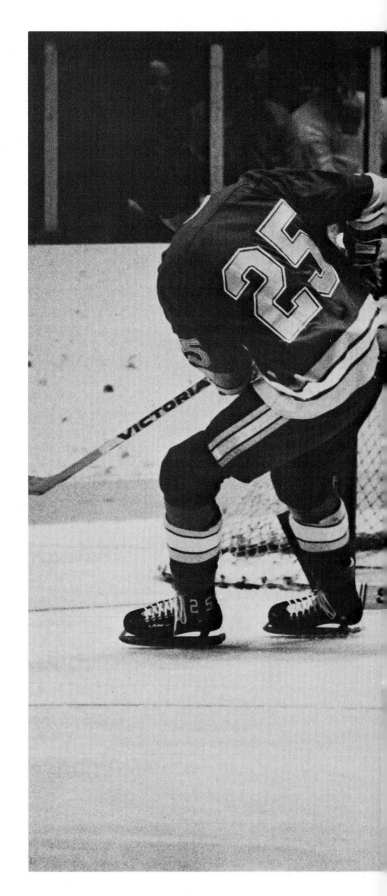

When an attacker speeds in on goal he tries to maneuver the goaltender into making the first move. The Rangers' Ed Giacomin has made the move—down —and the St. Louis Blues' Chuck Lefley shoots the puck into the net.

erally and wide enough so that he can push it into the empty twine.

While stickhandling frequently produces classic looking goals, the most common scores come about from any number of plain shooting maneuvers.

The traditional shot, the wrist drive, is usually most effective when taken from distances up to 25 feet from the net. It is launched by cradling the puck at the end of the stick blade and firing with a quick crack of the wrist in the direction of the goal. It is the most accurate shot available to the attacker, but frequently is eschewed in favor of the more flamboyant slap shot.

Deplored by many hockey instructors because of its erratic qualities, the slap shot nevertheless has become the most popular of all hockey shots. It is very similar in form to the traditional drive in golf. The player draws back his stick in the manner of a golfer striking the ball and then wallops the puck, following through as a duffer would on the green. The essential advantage of the slap shot, curiously, is also its disadvantage. It lacks accuracy but because of its uncertain direction frequently baffles and frightens goaltenders. The excitement of the slap shot is derived from the loud report as the flying stick crashes against the six ounce vulcanized rubber puck which then frequently echoes a second loud report as it caroms off the end boards.

A major advantage of the slap shot is that it generates great speed to the puck from dis-

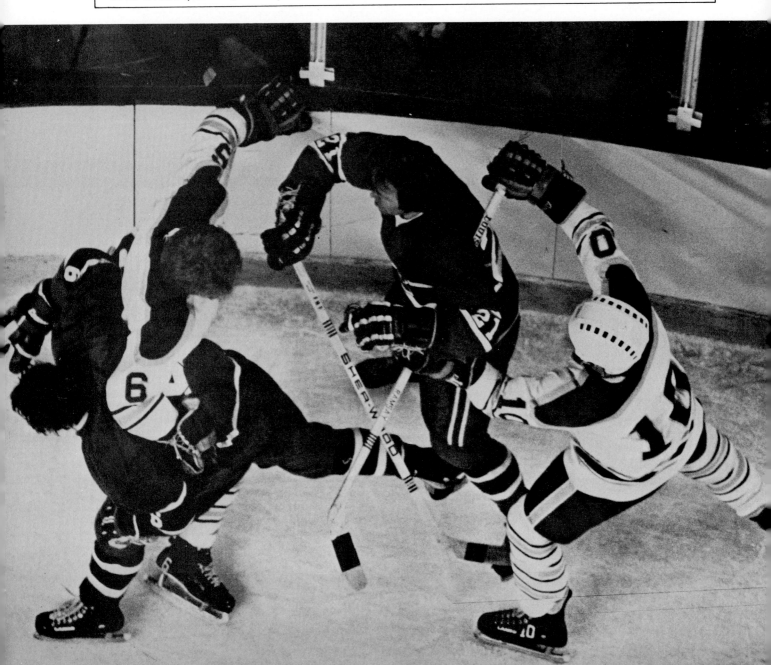

tances far from the goal. While it's unheard of for a wrist shooter to score a goal from center right, it is not uncommon for slap shooters to drill the puck home from distances as far as 90 feet from the net. This was decisively illustrated by a relatively unknown rookie named Bobby Schmautz who zoomed a shot from the center of Madison Square Garden ice past New York Rangers' goalie Ed Giacomin. Schmautz's slap shot turned out to be the vital score in a series won by Chicago. It indicated that even lesser lights could puncture a goalie's armor from afar.

Compounding the effectiveness of the slap shot was the advent of the curved or banana blade stick. Players who used the curve and slapped the puck were able to deliver shots that took sudden dives resembling the crazy and uncertain behavior of a knuckle ball.

More traditional is the backhand shot which like the forehand wrist shot has lost favor. The backhand is delivered from the side opposite the player's normal shooting position. Like the wrist shot it is released after being cradled on the blade of the stick. Again, a quick snap of the wrist propels the rubber on its way.

Quite often individual stickhandling and shooting are insufficient to produce goals. That's where play making comes in. The success of the 1974 and 1975 Stanley Cup champion Philadelphia Flyers was rooted in their offensive play making ability. Rather than accent individual efforts, the Flyers relied on play making, passing the puck up the ice from one free player to another.

In its most basic form play making is equated with puck control, keeping the rubber on your team's stick and not the enemy's.

The next step involved is getting the puck into attacking position. The most direct approach and one constantly employed by the Montreal Canadiens is called "head manning" the puck—passing it to a free man ahead of the original puck carrier. The recipient then looks for a teammate ahead of him and forwards the puck to him.

From this strategy there evolve several more complex alternatives culminating in intricate checkerboard maneuvers all with one basic premise in mind—keeping the puck away from the enemy.

A bastardized version of play making involves the "dump and run technique," in which the skater carries the puck over the center red line and then dumps it into the corner. The hope is that a teammate will outrace the enemy for the puck and then be able to feed a pass that will put a shooter in scoring position.

Traditional play making calls for each player to more or less stay in his respective lane. Thus the center generally orchestrates the plays for his left wing, who operates in the left alley, and the right wing, who skates on the opposite side of the rink.

Traditionally, the center is supposed to be a fluid skater with the ability to stickhandle as well as pass. His wing men, who also are expected to stickhandle with ease, actually are counted on to do more heavy shooting than the center. This unwritten rule is frequently broken and many centers score well.

Likewise, defensemen traditionally have been expected to concentrate on defending in an area behind their blue line. Thus the nickname—blueliners. However, over the years, defensemen have become effective puck carriers. Both a left defenseman and a right defenseman are apt to find themselves in the attacking zone on the opposite side from which they are normally expected to operate.

A basic function of the defenseman is to keep the area in front of his goalie free of threatening shooters. Usually, one of the defensemen will station himself in front of the goal while the other will operate either behind the net or wherever the threatening puck carrier might be.

Ideally, the goalie, defensemen and forwards should operate as a coordinated unit. Theoretically, the goaltender should be able to field the puck and move it ahead to a defenseman. The defenseman in turn should then shift the puck ahead to any one of his three forwards. This teammate to teammate operation in which one player helps another from a different position is essential to winning hockey.

The corners, called "the pits," are the roughest and often the most vital sections of the rink. Here, left to right, Jim Roberts of Montreal, Jim Schoenfeld of Buffalo, Glen Sather of Montreal and Craig Ramsay of Buffalo battle for control of a corner. Control of the corners often means control of the puck—and the game.

The face-off is both a very delicate and a vital aspect of the game. The player who can outwit his foe and win the draw is in a position to set up a teammate for a shot on goal. Bobby Clarke (No. 16), captain of the Philadelphia Flyers, has beaten Boston's Phil Esposito to the puck while Bobby Orr (No. 4) of the Bruins looks on. Clarke, now in control of the disk, will attempt to backhand it to a waiting shooter. The linesman is veteran Matt Pavelich.

To gain an advantage at a face-off, opposing centers try to anticipate the linesman's moves as he prepares to drop the puck. A split second move can mean the difference between winning and losing a hockey game if the face-off is correctly interpreted and won. Rick MacLeish (No. 19) of the Philadelphia Flyers and Ed Westfall (No. 18) of the New York Islanders lock sticks after the puck is dropped.

Face-Offs

Every hockey game begins with a face-off and some end as the result of a face-off.

The game's opening face-off occurs when the referee drops the puck between the two opposing centers. This is also done at the start of each of the other two periods. Subsequent face-offs are held at any one of the five face-off circles or four face-off spots on the rink, depending upon the site of play stoppage.

One of the two linesmen in the game drops the puck for the face-offs that take place after the initial drops.

Holding the puck in the palm of his hand, the referee or linesman does his best to drop the rubber biscuit accurately between the opposing sticks. He is careful to avoid causing the puck to bounce, as best he can, and does this with a twist of his hand as he releases the puck. Hopefully, this produces a flat or non-bouncing drop.

When they take their positions for the face-off, the opposing players are expected to line up in a legal formation; that is, all players except the two face-off men must remain outside the perimeter of the face-off circle. If the puck is dropped and the linesman or referee detects an infraction, a whistle is blown and the face-off is tried again.

The most effective face-off men in hockey in the 1970s—Bobby Clarke of Philadelphia and Derek Sanderson of the Rangers—are masters of concentration and students of various linesmen's techniques for dropping the puck. Carefully, they eye their opponent's stick and the linesman's hand and coordinate their movements to pull the puck away from their foe. Some win face-offs by making magical use of the stick, while others like to play the man, charging at their opponent when the puck is dropped and thereby removing him from play so a teammate can grab the rubber.

In hockey it is often necessary for a player to reverse ice rapidly and violently. To do so, he must first come to a complete stop even though he may be traveling at speeds of up to 35 miles per hour. He does this by jamming his skates into the ice and immediately reversing his direction. In this closeup, Rod Gilbert of the Rangers is doing just that.

The Importance of Skating

Down through the years, the most successful hockey teams have been those with the most agile skaters. Montreal's venerated Flying Frenchmen set the trend early, with the speedy Howie Morenz. The speed tradition carried through the seventies when the Canadiens iced a team of modern Morenzes, featuring such lightning-like skaters as Yvan "The Roadrunner" Cournoyer, Jacques Lemaire and Guy Lafleur. En route to two consecutive Stanley Cup championships, the Philadelphia Flyers utilized the superior skating of forwards Bobby Clarke and Rick MacLeish. Likewise, Buffalo's dipsy-doodling Sabres offered some of the speediest skaters in hockey history with their French Connection line of Gil Perreault, Rene Robert and Richard Martin.

Each of these aces learned to skate in his pre-teen years on Canadian rinks. To reach the top they had to master basic strokes. First and foremost was the art of power skating. Power skating is a technique which provides the player with the thrust to catapult himself into the action whether he is pursuing the puck or another player. It is accomplished by digging the blade of the skate into the ice and then pushing off powerfully with the foot.

When directing an attack from behind one's goal the skater must make a turn. This turn is similar to one that might be made at center ice or for that matter any part of the rink when direction is to be reversed. It involves a very important skating maneuver known as the cross step, in which the player crosses one leg over the other and pushes off—or perhaps jumps off the rear leg.

Because most players learn to skate in indoor rinks they tend to cross the right leg over the left much easier than left over right since the direction of flow of the skaters in rinks is counter-clockwise. This flaw is more pronounced on players who have not had the opportunity to free skate on outdoor rinks.

Another essential skating technique, especially for defensemen, is back skating. When a defenseman is confronted by an attack from within the enemy zone he frequently will (a) face the attackers to size up the situation, then (b) wheel around turning his back to them, skate several strides to pick up speed, then wheel around the second time to confront them again. Back skating at this juncture involves synchronized movements of the hip and skates, both hips moving back and forth producing reverse motion. A defenseman who has not mastered back skating is extremely vulnerable to sprints around his flanks.

The attacking skater should be able to employ several variations on the cross step to confound the defenseman. For example, he might, in a one-on-one situation, cross his left skate over his right pretending to make a run around the

Few accomplished forwards combine the skills of outstanding stickhandling, shooting and passing in almost equal proportions. One of those who has reached that level of excellence is Guy Lafleur of the Canadiens.

The lyrical beauty of a hockey player in motion is vividly demonstrated by Bill Fairbairn, the Rangers' veteran forward.

right side, but suddenly bring his right skate over his left to reverse ice, in what is known as a "deke," or fake, thus leaving the defenseman caught in his tracks.

If a defender, however, is an equally accomplished skater he will be able to adjust to a split second fake and while back skating be able to move his left skate over his right, to turn with and stop the attacker.

Whether it be power skating, back skating or any of the other skating nuances the art is mastered only by constant practice. Only a handful of mediocre skaters have made it to the big time. Those who have not are legion. It has been said, and with good reason, that the name of the game is skating.

Right: *There is a fine line between legal and illegal holding depending on the proximity of the referee. Rangers' defenseman Gilles Marotte manages to thrust his right hand in the way of Flyers' forward Bill Clement while nailing Clement's hand to the protective glass with his left arm. The referee is far enough away, so the play will continue. Otherwise two minutes to Marotte for holding. Clement joined the Washington Capitals after the close of the 1974-75 season.*

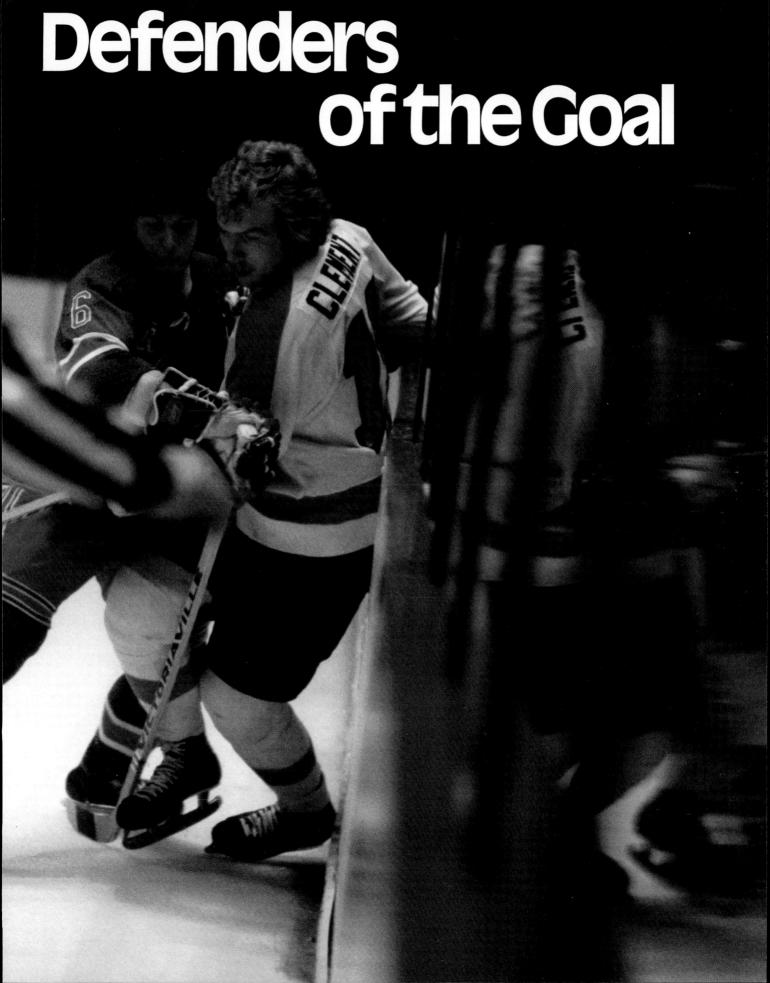

Defenders
of the Goal

The two-on-one break: Buffalo Sabres' captain Jim Schoenfeld (left) blasts over the blue line with teammate Don Luce in order to outflank a lone New York Islanders' defender. In the traditional cat-and-mouse game between the attacker and defender, Schoenfeld releases his pass a split second before his foe attempts a poke check, skimming the puck to the breaking Luce.

Notorious for his brutish play, Philadelphia Flyers' bad man Dave ''The Hammer'' Schultz can also be an effective scorer. Schultz surprised his critics by scoring a very respectable twenty goals during the 1973-74 season. When he concentrates on attacking the puck, Schultz can be a dangerous offensive player.

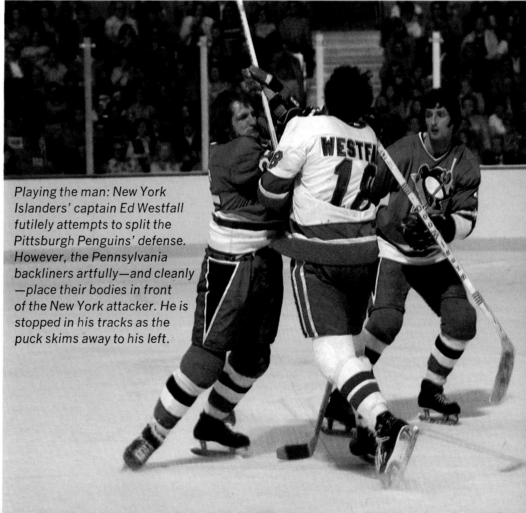

Top Right: *No matter how heavy the attack, the defenders must keep, or at least try to keep, the road clear in front of the net. Philadelphia Flyers' defenseman Andre Dupont does just that to an intruding Rangers' forward Bert Wilson. Dupont first smashes Wilson to the ice, allowing goalie Bernie Parent some viewing space and then attempts to push Wilson to the side. It is effective but not precisely legal.*

Playing the man: New York Islanders' captain Ed Westfall futilely attempts to split the Pittsburgh Penguins' defense. However, the Pennsylvania backliners artfully—and cleanly—place their bodies in front of the New York attacker. He is stopped in his tracks as the puck skims away to his left.

The most effective method of cleanly stopping an enemy along the boards is by thrusting the hip and shoulder against the opponent's body. This is vividly demonstrated by a New York Islander who stops a member of the Buffalo Sabres right in his tracks.

Even in its mildest form hockey is never gentle. Pittsburgh defenseman Ron Stackhouse efficiently takes Islander forward J. P. Parise out of play with a chest-thrust body check and then applies the crusher with a two-handed one stick shot in the shoulder. If there is a referee in the vicinity, Stackhouse will be called for interference.

Top Left: *Barclay Plager, the venerable St. Louis Blues' defenseman prepares to hop over the boards and enter the play.*

Below Left: *Off and running. Montreal Canadiens' defenseman Serge Savard picks up speed, after circling behind his net, for a charge up ice. Savard pushes the puck forward with his right hand grasping the stick, keeping his left hand in a defensive position to fend off enemy attackers. Savard uses his left skate for propulsion, bringing his right skate over the top of his left in a technique that hockey players like to call "jumping."*

For years hockey observers have been wondering when the National Hockey League would produce a successor to the fleet skating of Bobby Orr. The New York Rangers' candidate for the late seventies is Ron Greschner who can shoot as hard as the best scorers and skate as powerfully as Orr.

Above: *A new leader of the Montreal Canadiens is mustachioed defenseman Larry Robinson here moving to the attack.*

Top Right: *Bobby Orr, perhaps the best and most agile skater in modern hockey, is said to have "16 speeds of fast."*

Bottom Right: *They call him Moose but Andre Dupont has the acceleration of a gazelle when he speeds to the attack.*

In this confrontation between speed and guile, speed triumphs as the New York Rangers' lightning-like forward Rick Middleton outflanks the crafty but slower Philadelphia Flyers' defenseman Ed Van Impe while Flyers' teammate, left wing Ross Lonsberry, observes the play.

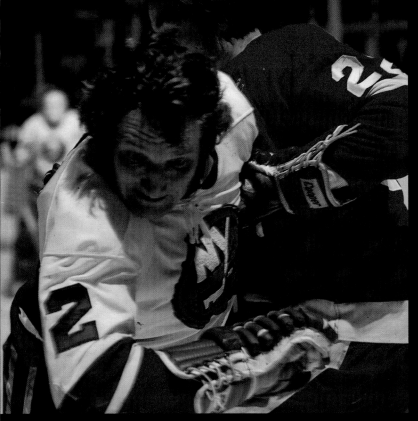

Left: The intensity of punishing play is reflected in the eyes of New York Islanders' defenseman Gerry Hart as he hustles past the enemy.

Below: Stan Weir of the California Seals betrays the anxiety of a forward put out of position as New York Rangers' defenseman Brad Park moves ahead of him into the clear.

Right: Jerry "King Kong" Korab, the bruising Buffalo Sabre, plays two hundred pounds of muscle against Philadelphia Flyers' forward Bill Barber during the 1975 Stanley Cup finals.

Below: Some of the nastiest play occurs along the side board. Ralph Stewart of the New York Islanders and Phil Russell of the Chicago Black Hawks pick up a sprinkling of snow as they smash full force into the wooden boards.

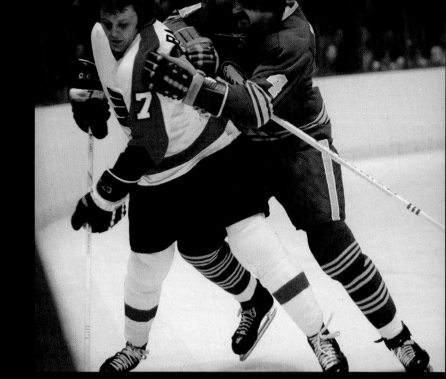

Crimson Ice

Left: You win some, you lose some; Boston Bruins' forward Terry O'Reilly has taken some notable decisions in hockey fights but this time pays the consequences as his bloodied face proves.

Below Center: When fighting appears to be an even match it is customary for the linesmen to let the players slug it out until one player appears to have the upper hand, or fist, as the case may be. Chicago Black Hawks' defenseman Keith Magnuson (right) appears to be scoring a technical knockout against Garry Howatt of the New York Islanders as the linesmen prepare to pry them apart.

Right: *It is incumbent upon the referee to keep his distance during a hockey fight so that he may ascertain which players are to be penalized. Meanwhile the linesmen are obliged to get right into the middle of the donnybrook and separate the combatants.*

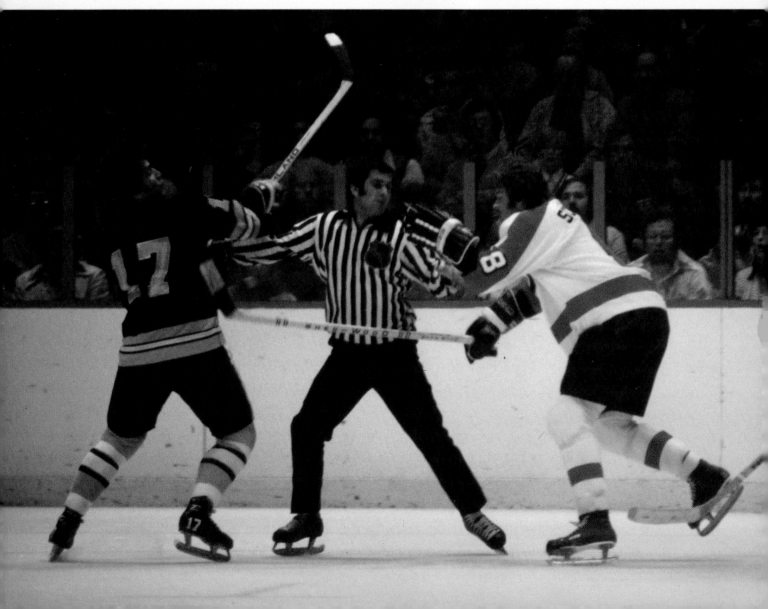

Far Left: *Hockey's law of the defensive jungle says that the goal crease must be kept clear of enemy forwards. During the 1974 Team Canada vs. Soviet series defenseman Rick Ley of the Canadian sextet effectively disposed of intruders in a less than gentle way.* Near Left: *Though commonplace in hockey, fights are eternally fascinating to players and fans alike. Ross Lonsberry of the Philadelphia Flyers and Brad Park of the New York Rangers go at it while team members stand on the bench and root for their side.*

Brawn, Brawls, Blood

Those who have studied hockey violence with a broad perspective dating back to the 19th century invariably point out that blood and ice are as closely linked as gin and vermouth. Violence is the natural consequence of fully grown men who are well armed, hurtling into each other at speeds of more than 25 miles per hour.

The result—crimson ice. Sometimes the bloodletting is an outgrowth of an accidental collision. After all, accidents *will* happen. At other times it's a result of a fistfight, inspired when one opponent rams another—illegally or otherwise.

"Fighting," says Philadelphia Flyers' coach Fred Shero, "is a natural consequence of events that have taken place on the hockey rink."

From the very beginning hockey leaders realized that robust play won more hockey games than Lord Fauntleroy behavior. Players were taught that the quickest way to the puck and on to the goal often was through or over an opponent. And if the opponent got tough, you'd have to get tougher.

From the time of the first fatality in a professional game in 1910 to this day, fighting has been a component of the game, even among very gifted stickhandlers.

There is usually one man on each team who is the policeman. He is the protector, the strong arm man. Often he can put so much fear into the hearts of his team's opponents that they are psyched away from their best play.

Once, in a game against the Boston Bruins, Stan Mikita of the Chicago Black Hawks indelicately massaged the Beantown favorite, Bobby Orr.

Mikita, a former displaced person who emigrated to Canada from Sokolce, Czechoslovakia, immediately was put on the Bruins' "most wanted" list. "When we see him next we'll ship him back to Czechoslovakia in a pine box," warned Boston coach Don Cherry.

A mortician wasn't necessary for Mikita but he got the message as did the Black Hawks' opponents when Mikita's teammate, Reg Fleming skated for Chicago on the last Black Hawk Stanley Cup winning team in 1961. In his day, Fleming was the roughest, toughest hombre in a Chicago uniform. He *had* to be, otherwise he wouldn't have made the team.

"In my first game in Chicago," Fleming remembers, "there was a brawl and I just sort of watched. In the dressing room, our coach Rudy Pilous said,

97

'Fleming, if your buddies are in trouble don't just stand there. Your job is to help them out, fight for them. If you don't, you might as well pack your bag, you're no use to us.' So I went out and fought. That was always my job. I didn't do it to be cruel, I was just following orders.''

Reggie Fleming, as much as any hockey player before or since, symbolized the hockey cop. He didn't get that way overnight. There was a long process of development as a child, then a teenager and, finally, as a professional. (Not surprisingly, Fleming was most influenced by Fred Shero when he played at Shawinigan Falls, Quebec.)

In Fleming's case, the basic training for becoming a hockey cop began on the sidewalks of his native Montreal. The survival ethic was spawned in a red brick house, from where Reggie, the altar boy, would go to church—and then fight.

"It was a tough neighborhood," Fleming explains. "English and French, mostly French and they were always attacking the English guys. You had to fight. I learned that you didn't back down. Guys would pick on me so I had to prove I was better than them. I had to fight better. I got a reputation as a fighter, a tough guy. But I only fought if challenged. You couldn't be a chicken.''

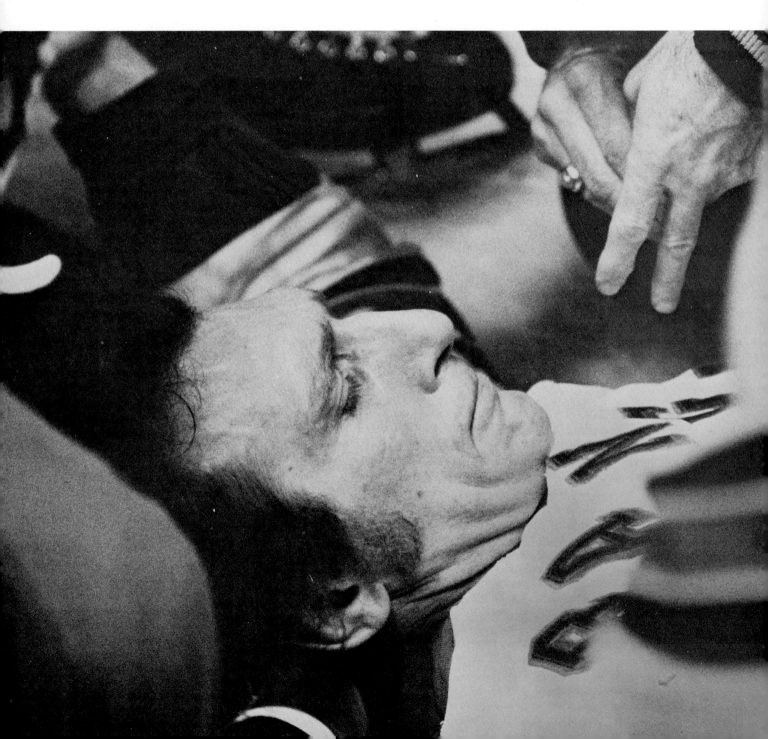

He carried his street smarts over to the hockey rink. Shero refined it for him in the minors and Pilous perfected it in the NHL. Naturally, Fleming didn't win *every* fight, but he won plenty and, he thinks, his teams were winners because of it. "The tough teams," he insists, "win the Stanley Cup."

As hockey cops go, Fleming was typical in size. He was muscular, built much like a light heavyweight boxer and his overall bulk was rather menacing. Not all hockey policemen are big. Garry Howatt of the New York Islanders is a little guy (five-feet-nine) as policemen go, yet he owns one of the best won-lost fight records in NHL history.

During the 1973–74 season, Howatt set an unofficial league record, engaging in 29 fights and losing very few of them. Howatt's development as a hockey pug was not unlike Fleming's, except that Garry grew up in Grand Center, Alberta. "Growing up," Howatt says, "I fought all the time. And we'd drink. Find us a bootlegger and go off somewhere and drink."

One Howatt watcher said that in those early days if a Brahma bull looked cross-eyed at Howatt, he'd let the bull have it, right between the horns.

The rodeo came to Grand Center one summer where Howatt had what he regards as his basic training in two-fisted fighting. "I was just walking by this bunch of cowboys," he recalls. "They'd been trying to pick fights with some of the younger kids. I said, 'Let 'em go.' This big oi' cowboy stepped out and gave me a slap.

"We went at it. Must have lasted 15, maybe 20 minutes. I cut him up pretty good. But he overpowered me. Didn't leave any marks. Mostly, he just kept hitting me in the head. Tired me out. He was the toughest guy I ever fought."

Sometimes Howatt's fights are spontaneous, at other times they are against members of his personal hate parade such as Philadelphia Flyers' captain Bobby Clarke.

"Clarke," snarls Howatt, "is always hitting after the whistle. He's always sticking guys."

Why would Clarke, a winner of the Hart Trophy as the NHL's most valuable player in the 1972–73 season, be regarded by Howatt and others as one of the dirtiest players in the league?

"It's an awful thing to carry around—that you're a dirty player," says Clarke. "The person responsible for what I consider unfair misrepresentation is

Scotty Bowman (the Montreal Canadiens' coach). When we first were in the play-offs with Montreal, Bowman apparently said that Bobby Clarke was the dirtiest player in the NHL. I've been stuck with it ever since.

"But it just isn't true. If I was as dirty as some people try to make out, I'd have had hell beaten out of me long before. My interpretation of a dirty hockey player is that he deliberately tries to hurt somebody."

Clarke tries so hard during a game it often is difficult to determine whether his infractions against any enemy skater are deliberate or accidental. As a member of Team Canada 1972, Clarke singled out Valery Kharlamov, the Russian ace, for destruction. With the Soviet team leading the series by two games, with only three to play, Clarke slashed the Russian across the ankles and sidelined Kharlamov for the remainder of that game and the entire next game. "It's not something I was really proud of," Clarke said later, "but I honestly can't say I was ashamed to do it."

Some critics excused Clarke on the grounds that the Russians were egregious sinners when it came to slashing, spearing and butt-ending. But others indict Clarke for spearing Toronto defenseman Rod Seiling in front of the net at Maple Leaf Gardens. "I deeply regret it," says Clarke in reflection. "This was a terrible thing—especially since Seiling is a friend. I called him the next day to apologize and I really was relieved when Rod told me he wasn't hurt. He saw the spear coming, he said, and was able to avoid it."

The Seiling-Clarke episode underlines a rule of the hockey jungle: friends off the ice are enemies on the ice. Such is the case with Clarke and New York Islanders' defenseman Gerry Hart. They are lifelong friends; they played together in junior hockey for the Flin Flon (Manitoba) Bombers and they make a point of getting together every summer back home in their native Flin Flon.

However, as Hart has said, once they start playing hockey against each other it's different. "I don't think it would be fair to either of us to show a friendly attitude so our friendship takes a back seat. We don't acknowledge each other's presence, not even with a nod," Hart says.

Howatt who also teamed with Clarke in Flin Flon says he once idolized Bobby but lost his admira-

Lying horizontally on the ice following an excruciatingly painful broken ankle, New York Rangers' defenseman Dale Rolfe receives sedation from the team trainer.

tion the more he analyzed Clarke's style. Even members of the Flyers have questioned the value of excessive violence and repeated fights.

Precisely what level of violence in big league hockey is acceptable remains a moot question and probably always will as long as there are pucks, sticks and elbows. Flyers' coach Fred Shero accuses other coaches of dispatching "hit men" to deliberately pick fights with his men and says, "If it doesn't happen as a natural consequence of the game, it's not right."

Sometimes events on the ice escalate to a degree of violence that frightens even law enforcement officials; and they worry that the virus of violence has spread far beyond the player. One of the most chilling displays occurred during the 1974–75 season when Dave Forbes of the Boston Bruins attacked Henry Boucha of the Minnesota North Stars.

In that incident, Forbes jammed the end of his stick into Boucha's right eye, leaving Boucha, after surgery, with impaired vision. In an unprecedented criminal action against an NHL player, Forbes was charged with aggravated assault with a dangerous weapon.

Members of the anti-violence clique argue that the Flyers' buccaneering play has inspired normally non-belligerent players to take arms. During the 1975 Stanley Cup play-offs, for example, Guy Lafleur, the normally peaceful Montreal Canadiens' scorer speared Jim Lorentz of the Buffalo Sabres for no apparent reason and received a five-minute major penalty.

Others say the fans have become as violent as the Flyers, and not only in the major leagues. In the wake of a Canadian amateur championship in 1975 fans in St. John's, Newfoundland, stormed the hotel at which the visiting Barrie Flyers were staying. About 35 people invaded the hotel, breaking some windows, in an attempt to assault the Barrie players.

In Quebec, Larry Regan, coach of the Montreal Juniors, was vilified by fans not too long ago when he refused to institute a policy of immediate counterattack against assaults of his skaters. Regan quit in disgust. "The overemphasis on violence," he said, "and the use of sticks has become so much a part of the league that that is now the only

way a team can win . . . Violence scares the good

It often takes two officials to cool off the Flyers' cop—Dave Schultz (No. 8) during a fight. Here, one holds Schultz while another tries to verbally soothe him as tempers flare behind them.

Everybody, as Jimmy Durante would say, wants to get into the act, especially hockey fans. While Bruins and Canadiens battle against the end boards at Boston Garden, fans lean into the action, encouraging their favorites from behind the glass partition.

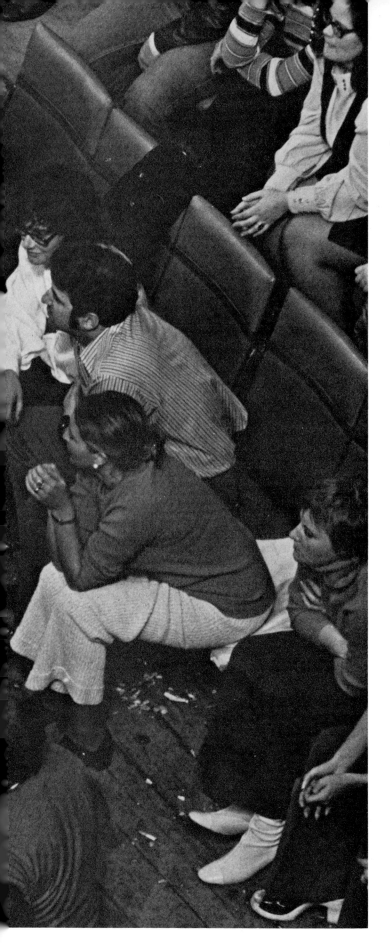

hockey player, and his development is held back. When I joined the team there was one fellow who couldn't play hockey. Fighting was all he was there for, so I didn't play him. I couldn't justify sending someone out to play to beat someone up in order to win ... I think a league needs some fights; there's nothing wrong with that, but for that to be all a fellow is out there for is a disgrace."

Blood on the ice is not always the result of a high stick in the neck or a slash on the ankle. The fast-flying puck—often a misguided missile—does more damage than a rock hard fist. Defensemen who hurl their bodies in front of the flying rubber often wind up in a hospital bed, wishing they had allowed the puck to fly past them.

Once, Detroit Red Wings' defenseman Bryan Watson nearly got killed in such a manner. "It was the worst I've ever seen," says Watson's former teammate Keith McCreary. "Bryan dove to block a shot, and he came up with the puck in his mouth. When they pulled the puck out, all his teeth came out with it."

But hockey players are cut from the very toughest athletic cloth. They often are impervious to injuries that would sideline less hardy performers. Dr. Gerald Reed, team dentist of the Atlanta Flames, offers as evidence the case of Flames' center Bob Leiter.

"One night," says Dr. Reed, "Bob was at the face-off circle and I saw blood dripping on the ice. He had broken three front teeth in half. It was considered so minor that I wasn't even called. He just kept on playing as if nothing had happened."

Likewise, hard-nosed hockey players rebound like tennis balls even when they lose a fight. Garry Howatt recalls the night he was pulverized by a seemingly endless collection of Philadelphia Flyers during the 1975 Stanley Cup semifinals.

"I got knocked on my butt," says Howatt. "The whole game I was up and down. Up and down. I felt like a damned yo-yo. But I'm not afraid to lose a a fight. There's always the next game. If I lose the fight but we win the game, that's okay. Lose the fight *and* the game, that's a real bummer!"

The Fight: *Most hockey fights begin with a spontaneous dropping of the gloves by the combatants. Each then attempts to gain an advantage, either by outslugging the foe, or by pulling his jersey over his head, thus neutralizing him, or just wrestling the enemy to the ice by sheer muscle force. This is vividly demonstrated as Rick Dudley overcomes Bob Kelly.*

A function of the linesmen is to separate battlers in a fight. The referee's job is to analyze the action and determine the penalty to be meted out to the player or players involved. Here, both Barclay Plager (No. 8) of St. Louis and Dennis Hextall of Minnesota will be sent off with five-minute major penalties for fighting.

Scapegoats of the Rink

Hockey referees and linesmen are somewhat like the poor sap at carnivals who sticks his head through a hole and lets people throw baseballs at him. They don't throw baseballs in hockey games but the spectators do hurl obscenities, voice threats and occasionally proffer a punch in the nose.

No official in any sport absorbs as much abuse as frequently as a hockey referee. This is due, in part, to the frontier philosophy that has permeated the game since its earliest days in the wilds of Canada. It also is due to the broad and loose interpretation of the rule book which, on one night will be interpreted with permissive liberality by one referee and on the next with rock hard, strict adherence to the letter of the law by another official.

As a result fans, players, coaches and managers have taunted and attempted to intimidate referees ever since the first puck was dropped and the first whistle was blown. Francis "King" Clancy, now a vice-president of the Toronto Maple Leafs, absorbed as much fan flak as any official who ever wore the black and white striped NHL referee's uniform.

One Boston Garden fan regularly greeted him as follows, "Hey, Clancy, we've got a town named after you. Marblehead."

On another night defenseman Babe Pratt of the Toronto Maple Leafs needled Clancy so much during the game, the referee finally exploded. "You big jerk, I'd love to be playing against you tonight," Clancy shouted at Pratt. To which Pratt shot back, "Well, aren't you?"

One time at Madison Square Garden a patriotic pre-game ceremony was ended with a volley of shots delivered by a squad of soldiers. Suddenly, a fan in the peanut gallery shouted: "When you get through with that—shoot Clancy!"

Clancy's problem was the same as it has been and will continue to be for all hockey referees: the game is too speedy and unplanned for one man to adequately officiate. As a result many infractions are lost in the maddening ebb and flow of play. Then, there are borderline infractions that make it difficult to determine whether a player was deliberately tripped (for which the referee should call a two minute penalty) or whether it was an accident and should be overlooked.

But fans couldn't care less. If the referee misses a penalty he immediately is confronted by the wrath of thousands of spectators with usually one leather lunged fan prepared to deliver the imperfect squelch.

Superficially, the referee would seem to have a relatively simple job. He functions, with the aid of two linesmen, for the entire 60 minutes of the game. Yet, he does little of the dirty work involved in a game. When a fight breaks out, for example, the referee moves back and allows the linesmen to separate the combatants.

While the linesmen supervise face-offs and retrieve lost pucks, the referee concerns himself with infractions that range from minor penalties (two minutes) to major penalties (five minutes) to the more serious misconduct infractions and game misconduct penalties.

Linesmen are available to "assist" referees during a game. If a referee overlooks a penalty but a linesman notices it, the linesman can advise the referee that an infraction should be whistled down. More often than not, linesmen prefer to stay away from the referee's sphere of influence with the result that one man rules the game.

Supervising all referees is the league (both NHL and WHA) referee-in-chief. His function is to assure a high quality of officiating by constantly monitoring the work of his men and evaluating the steady stream of criticism that envelops referees from week to week.

During the 1975 Stanley Cup semifinal round between the Montreal Canadiens and Buffalo Sabres, Canadiens' coach Scotty Bowman delivered a typical broadside at the officials. Claiming that referee Lloyd Gilmour had favored the Sabres over the Canadiens, Bowman confronted Ian (Scotty) Morrison the NHL referee-in-chief outside the dressing rooms.

The two engaged in a shouting match viewed by newsmen, hordes of fans and game officials. "You don't like me," snapped Bowman.

"What do you mean I don't like you?" countered Morrison. "What do I have to do, write love letters to you? Does your club ever lose a goddamn game by itself?"

Cooler heads intervened, until the next game when the needles between coaches and referees flew again. Less noticeable are the exchanges between referees and players which occur constantly as play moves up and down a rink. Usually the referee–player dialogue goes unrecorded. But in 1975 a couple of referees—one from the NHL, Ron Wicks, and another from the WHA, Wayne Mundey—were equipped with microphones and wallet-sized transmitters strapped to their waists where players couldn't see them, each one for a single game. Their conversations were then recorded for posterity on a tape machine in the Maple Leaf Gardens press box.

At one point in a Bruins–Leafs game Boston defenseman Carol Vadnais believed that referee Wicks had blown the whistle too quickly when Wicks lost sight of the puck along the boards.

"What are you doing, ref?" Vadnais shouted.

"Well, Jesus," Wicks shot back, "I'm not Clark Kent. From where I am, I can't see the puck. I have no alternative. I must blow the whistle."

The episode produced a typically embarrassing situation for the referee. He had blown his whistle too quickly (although technically, he had done the right thing since he *had* lost sight of the puck) and on the next face-off, Toronto got the puck and scored.

A referee can be the loneliest man in the rink, especially when his call angers some of the skaters. To protect himself from complainers the official can skate behind a semicircle near the penalty timekeeper's bench. Any skater who intrudes on that area is susceptible to an additional penalty. Here Buffalo Sabres' skaters register their disapproval of an official decision. A hundred times out of a hundred the referee cannot be persuaded to change his mind.

Referees generally mesh gears smoothly with their linesmen. In the NHL game, Wicks had his eyes on the constant jostling of Terry O'Reilly of Boston and Tiger Williams of Toronto, both notorious fighters. Wicks skated over to his linesmen and warned: "They'll go before the night's over."

At another point the referee detected what he believed to be an illegal maneuver by Boston's Wayne Cashman. Wicks alerted his linesman Claude Bechard to be aware of a similar maneuver in front of the enemy net.

"Cashman faces the blue line and tries to deflect the puck into the net with his skates . . . You watch him when he's near the net. Some night it'll save a lot of trouble because he does it. He tried it twice tonight. He's facing the blue line, the puck comes by and he moves his feet. So it hits his skate—no goal!"

On seven out of ten penalties some form of protest is registered by players or coaches. Referees expect complaints and generally ignore them or squelch the complainer as succinctly as possible. "Booing the officials is part of the game," says Ron Asselstine who has emerged as one of the toughest WHA officials.

It was Asselstine's toughness that convinced WHA referee-in-chief Vern Buffey that Ron would make a good official. Buffey was scouting a junior hockey game in Peterborough, Ontario, in which Ron was a linesman.

Flyers' defenseman Andre Dupont and Sabres' forward Peter McNab reflect the tension of a play-off game.

"I was in the officials' dressing room after the game talking to Asselstine," Buffey relates, "and suddenly there's this banging on the door. Some fan is trying to get at the officials. Asselstine opens the door—he's only got a towel on—and tells them if they kick it again, he'll come out after them. They're big guys, too. Five of them, in their 20s and 30s, leather jackets, tough looking. They went away and the officials finished dressing.

"As we're leaving the arena, these guys catch up with us. They're after the referee. But Ron steps in front of them and says if they want the referee, they'll have to go through him. The biggest guy grabbed Ron's jacket, and Ron let him have it. One punch in the face. Knocked the guy out cold. 'Okay,' he says, 'who's next?' Nobody moved. This guy was *out*—he didn't wake up for 40 minutes.

"I knew then and there I had to hire Ron. He could *handle* himself."

Asselstine was hired and, in a typical season, travels as much as any big league official: 120,000 miles to handle 100 games in an eight-month period. Like other big, tough linesmen (John D'Amico is one of the NHL's best), Asselstine uses his size and strength to advantage in breaking up a fight on the ice. "If you're in a fight on the ice," says Buffey, "and he grabs you, you've had it."

Linesmen use their discretion in breaking up fights. If they believe the two battlers are evenly matched, they'll allow them to slug it out until they feel both have suitably spent their energy. Then each will try to grab one battler to insure that neither has an advantage in swinging free to hit the other while the peacemaking process is taking place.

Occasionally a player will lose his temper and threaten a linesman. It has happened to every one of them. "We're out there to keep the peace not fight with the players," says Asselstine, "but once in a game at Houston I had trouble. It happened after I had given a player a ten-minute misconduct for swinging at me, and as he was heading for the penalty box, he put his stick across my chest. We're not supposed to threaten anybody, but I said, 'Get that stick off me, or they'll carry you out of here in an orange crate.'

"Luckily, for both of us, he did."

Sometimes, even hockey's scapegoats come out on top.

Penalties

Hockey is probably the most difficult game to officiate accurately because of the fine line that exists between a foul, a legal body check and a stick check. Since mayhem—crunching body against body—is legalized to a point, officials frequently find it impossible to make a distinction between an honest and a dishonest check. Elbowing, and a two-minute penalty, to one referee may be nothing more than a robust belt in the mouth to another. When one whistle blower calls a penalty for tripping, another will argue that it wasn't tripping at all, but rather that the so-called victim was "taking a swan dive."

Whatever the case, penalties can be broken down into two basic categories—the severe and the innocuous. A severe penalty is anything that ranges from a five minute major to a ten minute misconduct to a game misconduct infraction. The less severe penalties are two minute "minors" which run the gamut from tripping through hooking and cross-checking to high-sticking. The infractions are virtually self-explanatory. A high-sticking infraction occurs when a player carrying his stick above his shoulder plants the lumber in or about his opponent's skull, shoulder or arm. Likewise, tripping is called when a man inserts his stick or leg in front of the opponent, causing him to fall on his face, his back or stomach. An elbowing penalty is usually called when the elbow is jammed into an enemy's face. Since the hockey stick is formed in a hook shape it is frequently used to "hook an enemy to a halt" by being under his armpit, over his shoulder, around his waist or occasionally, in cases of near decapitation, around his neck. That calls for a hooking penalty.

Usually, these are whistled down as minor or two minute infractions, which means the culprit, like a naughty boy, must sit alone in the penalty box (alias *sin bin*) for two minutes. However, if the enemy should score while he is

Referees often get the impression that they might as well talk to the wall as to get players to observe the rules. Art Skov, who retired after the 1974-75 season, is not talking to the wall here; he is announcing a penalty to the time-keeper.

sitting out his penalty he is let out immediately.

If the infraction is of a more serious nature, i.e., if a smashing elbow draws enemy blood, the assailant is given a five minute major penalty. This means he must remain in the hoose-gow for the full five minutes no matter how many goals are scored against his team.

Misconduct penalties, the ten minute variety, are frequently called for verbal abuse of the officials. The game misconduct penalty, in which the offending party is tossed out of the match, is an extension of the misconduct. In the NHL, a game misconduct is automatically called if a third player intrudes upon a fight involving two others (the third man rule).

Since penalties occur in almost every hockey game it is incumbent upon each team to provide an effective penalty killing unit. This group consists of a few players who are able to maintain control of the puck until their team gets back to full strength or who are able to blunt the opposition with poke checks and assorted body blocks.

A typical penalty killing unit features two defensemen and one forward with special skating skills and another who is an expert fore-checker. The skater will attempt to keep control of the puck as long as he can and then "ice" the puck into deep enemy territory. His fore-checking teammate then would try to zero in on the rubber and harass the enemy before they can launch a counterattack.

Some teams believe that the best defense against a power play is a good offense. Teams such as the Boston Bruins frequently will insert their best shooters such as Phil Esposito as penalty killers. An Esposito or a Bobby Clarke is because of his many attack approaches, able to keep the enemy at bay by attacking rather than defending against the power play.

Although the penalty is supposed to be a form of punishment, hockey teams, through the years, have discovered that illegal play often intimidates the opposition and reaps rewards. What better example than the Philadelphia Flyers and their chief ruffian Dave "the Hammer" Schultz. In 1974 and 1975 the Flyers and Schultz broke almost every conceivable individual and team penalty record in the book. Yet they won the Stanley Cup in both years.

Policemen

Every hockey team has a right wing and a left wing also known as forwards, a center, a goaltender, two defensemen and—a policeman. No, not seven players; the ice cop is often one of the defensemen.

The policeman is usually unofficially designated by the coach or manager to enforce order in his team's favor. If an opponent abus-

Big Jim Schoenfeld, Buffalo's young captain, lets the Flyers' Gary Dornhoefer feel his full weight at the boards as he wraps his arm around Dornhoefer to further impede his progress. The result is two minutes for holding.

Sometimes it is impossible for a defenseman such as Brad Park of the New York Rangers (No. 2) to body check an opponent cleanly without "laying on the lumber." In this case Park is nailing a Toronto forward while eyeing the elusive puck.

More than any other contact sport hockey is probably the most bruising. Here, Montreal's big defenseman Larry Robinson, who has five inches and fifteen pounds on Rod Gilbert, raps Rod's head with his elbow.

Burly St. Louis defenseman Bob Plager is notorious for his destructive body checks but he has also developed into a worthy puck carrier.

es a teammate, the ice cop is expected to intervene on behalf of his teammate sometime during the game. Intervention can take the form of a stern warning or a punch in the mouth.

Normally the hockey policeman is one of the biggest and toughest members of the squad—although not necessarily the most flamboyant or loudest. Ted Harris and Orland Kurtenbach spoke quietly but carried big fists when each filled the position for the Montreal Canadiens and the Toronto Maple Leafs, respectively.

Unlike Harris and Kurtenbach, Dave Schultz of the Philadelphia Flyers, the most notorious ice cop on the seventies' scene, is given to frequent outbursts of temper. As a result Schultz is penalized as much for his anti-referee tantrums as he is for his battles with the opposition.

Opinions vary widely about the effectiveness of the policemen. Some hockey theorists believe that it is impossible for a team to win a championship without a strong law and order man to "keep the enemy honest." Yet, when the Montreal Canadiens won the Stanley Cup in 1973 they did so without their feared policeman, Johnny Ferguson, who had retired from active play.

How do ice cops get that way?

For some, it comes naturally. Ferguson admittedly was an awkward skater and mediocre shooter when the Canadiens imported him from Cleveland and the American League. "I was there," says Ferguson, "to make sure that the other teams didn't push around our aces such as Jean Beliveau and Yvan Cournoyer—the guys who didn't do as much fighting. If anyone tried to mess with them, it was my job to move in."

For others it doesn't come naturally; they have to be ordered to be cops. After Ferguson retired, the Canadiens needed another enforcer. Big Pierre "Butch" Bouchard appeared to be the most likely successor to Ferguson. But Bouchard's personality was more like that of Ferdinand the Bull. He preferred a more tranquil game although when properly infuriated he was dynamite with his dukes. The Cana-

diens made it clear that Bouchard would have to switch—and fight. This he did, scoring impressive triumphs over the likes of Dave Schultz and the ferocious Flyers. But Bouchard preferred it otherwise and eventually got his way. The Canadiens hired Doug Risebrough, a young slugger who would just as soon bop an enemy as score a goal, both of which he did.

The majority of the fighters—the ice cops—are muscular brutes, taller and heavier than the ordinary hockey player. There are, however, some notable exceptions.

Bryan "Superpest" Watson, the Detroit Red Wings' defenseman, is one of the smaller (five-feet-ten, 170 pounds) backliners in the business, yet he is one of the first to come to the aid of a teammate and involve himself in a brawl. With Watson it's a visceral reaction. It's the same with Schultz and Ferguson.

So, policemen would appear to be an integral part of the game and probably always will be as long as hockey is played.

Protectors of the Law

The sentinels of the hockey rink are the referee and two linesmen.

As supervisor of the entire rink, the referee not only whistles all infractions of the rules (he can also be advised to call a penalty by a linesman), but he has the authority to overrule a goal judge or any other minor official, such as the penalty timekeeper or official scorer.

Referees launch the game with a face-off at center ice and then keep their eyes open for potential penalties. Linesmen are assigned to whistle offsides and line infractions such as icing the puck, which occurs when a team shoots the puck from their side of the center red line across the end goal line.

Linesmen are also employed to intervene during scuffles and physically break up fights. Referees, as a rule, do not involve themselves in the bouts other than to stand aside and decide which players are to get penalties and the extent of the penalties.

Officiating at games is enormously taxing. Unlike players who are relieved every three or four minutes, the referees and linesmen are required to skate without relief for the entire 60 minutes of a game. Unless a referee or linesman is seriously injured, he makes a point of following the rule that "the show must go on."

Few of the best hockey players have become competent referees. One of the rare exceptions was Frank "King" Clancy, a crack defenseman for the Toronto Maple Leafs who became a widely respected NHL arbiter before turning in his whistle to become an executive with the Toronto Maple Leafs organization.

Referees such as Clancy believe in the "broad and loose" school of interpreting the rule book. King, like many present day officials such as Lloyd Gilmour of the NHL, enjoyed a robust game and tended to overlook borderline penalties which certainly would have been called by his colleagues.

Some officials follow a "strict construction" of the rule book doctrine. These officials theorize that it is important to crack down on offenders early in the game to maintain decorum and gain respect from skaters on both teams.

There can be no such flexibility for linesmen calling offsides. Although there are close plays at the line, a skater, in the linesman's eyes, is either offside or onside and should be whistled appropriately.

Linesmen are selected not only for their speed and their accuracy in interpreting the rules but also for their strength. The ability to separate a pair of 200 pound brawlers frequently demands extraordinary powers of persuasion and "musculinity."

Once a penalty is whistled by the referee, the offending player is required to take the shortest possible route to the penalty box.

A special area is provided for each team in the penalty box section. Normally, two or three bench spaces are provided in each penalty box as well as room for the penalty timekeepers who see to it that the players are released at the precise moment that their penalty time elapses.

In cases of multiple penalties, the referee and penalty timekeepers must coordinate their signals to make sure that players are not retained in the box longer than their apportioned sentences, nor for less time than penalized.

In addition to a penalty timekeeper the referee is assisted in officiating at matches by a timekeeper who is in charge of the electronic clock and a manual stopwatch, an official scorer who records goals and assists and two goal judges, one behind each net, who push the button that activates the red light when the puck enters the net and a goal is scored.

It is one of the oddities of big league hockey that despite the importance and intensity of their jobs none of the minor officials—timekeeper, scorer, penalty timekeeper, goal judges—are paid a salary. Each of these jobs is a labor of love.

A defenseman must be able to stickhandle or pass his way out of any kind of surrounding threat. Montreal Canadiens' defenseman Guy Lapointe seems to be trapped by three members of the California Seals. However, LaPointe has an option to manipulate the puck around the attackers and pass it up ice or stickhandle it out of his defensive zone.

Darryl Sittler (No. 27), the Maple Leaf's crack scorer, is momentarily blocked by the Minnesota defense.

The Defensive Game

"DEE-FENSE! DEE-FENSE!!"

The roars of the crowds cascading down from the balconies of arenas across the North American continent are pleas for the home club to reinforce its trenches on the ice and blunt the enemy attacks.

Ever since the inception of hockey, defensemen have been the unsung heroes of the game. There have been exceptions to be sure—Bobby Orr, Eddie Shore and Babe Pratt, all of whom have basked in the spotlight of publicity—but generally defenders have done their work in the shadows of the more spectacular goal scoring forwards and the punting, sprawling, kicking goaltenders.

"The reason we weren't noticed," said Ching Johnson, one of the NHL's greatest defensemen, a New York Ranger from 1926 through 1937 and a member of the Hockey Hall of Fame, "was because in those days a defenseman was supposed to play defense."

Johnson, like Taffy Abel, Leo Bourgault and others of the old-time hockey pros concentrated on defending their goal. They rarely ventured into the attacking zone on offensive forays and took the greatest delight in body checking the enemy with shoulder or hip—or both.

In a typical defensive situation, the two backliners would stand at the blue line and, literally, dare the attackers to pass them. Some of the most exciting challenges of pro hockey in the twenties and thirties involved a one-on-one situation in which a forward would attempt to bypass a defenseman.

More than anything, defensemen took enormous pride in leveling the enemy with violent body checks and no one did it better, or more enthusiastically, than Ching Johnson.

"Ching loved to deliver a good hoist early in a game," said his former teammate Frank Boucher, a Ranger from 1926 through 1944, "because he knew his victim would most likely retaliate. And Ching loved body contact."

One night in a game against the Montreal Maroons Ching nailed Hooley Smith with a lusty body check at the start of the game. It was the kind of check that helped sell hockey to the spectators in the game's early days in the United States.

"Hooley's stick flew from his hands and disappeared above the rink lights," Boucher continued. "He was lifted clean off the ice and seemed to stay suspended five or six feet above the surface for seconds before finally crashing down on his back. 119

In the aftermath of an attack, Rick Middleton of the Rangers slides to the ice against the hip of Canadiens' defenseman Serge Savard. Meanwhile, Ken Dryden deftly pokes away the puck with his large goalie stick.

Chicago defenseman Keith Magnuson sweeps away from the corner, his eyes glued to the puck. Magnuson, by concentrating on the rubber, is leaving himself open to an attack from his blind side.

"No one could accuse Hooley of lacking guts. From then on, whenever he got the puck he drove straight for Ching, trying to outmatch him, but each time Ching flattened poor Hooley. Afterwards, grinning in the shower, Ching said he couldn't remember a game he'd enjoyed more."

Unlike Johnson, Eddie Shore of the Bruins was more of a puck carrier—rare for a defenseman in the late twenties—although he reveled in the heavy traffic. It has been said that Shore collected more than 600 stitches during his long career.

Because of his long, powerful strides, Shore was able to sprint rapidly from one end of the rink to the other. If his attempted assault against the enemy goal failed, he would double back to his blue line post, often arriving there before the counterattackers could move into proper formation.

But Shore was the exception. Even in the late thirties, defensemen stuck to defense. Walter "Babe" Pratt, another good skater and shooter, hardly ever took the kind of excursions for which Shore was famous. Pratt's forte was sticking out his rear end, sort of sideways, and tipping the attacking player over his feet.

Another formidable body checker of the late thirties and early forties was Bucko McDonald who delighted in bouncing onrushing forwards off his abundant chest. His onetime Toronto Maple Leafs' teammate Bingo Kampman was another blocker of enormous strength. In his spare time Kampman liked to take heavy oak tables in his mouth and lift them off the ground by clenching his teeth and standing upright.

McDonald and Kampman were eventually victimized by a dramatic change in the game's style of play. Little by little defensive defensemen were becoming almost as extinct as the dodo bird. Bingo and Bucko got their comeuppance during the 1942 Stanley Cup finals between the Leafs and Red Wings.

Instead of attempting to carry the puck around the Toronto defenders in traditional style, the Detroit skaters shot the rubber into the corner of the rink as they approached the Maple Leafs' blue line. When the bulky McDonald and Kampman attempted to conduct an orderly retreat into the corners for the puck, they discovered that the speedy Red Wings had whipped around them and, on the end run, had snared the puck before Bingo and Bucko could get there.

The strategy worked so well that the Red Wings won three games in a row. Kampman and McDonald were benched, and the Leafs reorganized their strategy and won the next four games and the Stanley Cup. Defensive hockey was never the same after that. The "dump-and-run" school of attacking meant that speedier defensemen would be needed.

By the late forties, the emphasis on attack became more pronounced and new defensive measures were needed to cope with the heavier shooting and increased use of the power play in which teams utilized five forwards (or four forwards and an offensive minded defenseman) during a man advantage situation, and proceeded to bombard the goaltender.

A pair of young Toronto defenders, Garth Boesch and Bill Barilko, devised an effective antidote to this kind of shooting gallery situation. Instead of allowing the shots to pour, unimpeded, at their goalie Turk Broda, Boesch and Barilko would drop to their knees in tandem the moment a shot was released.

The synchronized drop, in effect, created a human wall which frequently deflected the pucks harmlessly away from the net. So effective was the Boesch-Barilko technique that other players began copying their style. The most effective single defender to refine the puck blocking move was Detroit defenseman Bob Goldham. Unlike the Leaf defensemen, Goldham would make his move alone. In time he achieved fame as *the* outstanding puck blocking defenseman and Boesch and Barilko were virtually forgotten.

Such maneuvers, however, were not without their hazards. Defenseman Bill Gadsby of the Rangers learned it the hard way during a 1954 game against the Boston Bruins. As a Bruins' defenseman launched a drive from the blue line, Gadsby flopped to the ice—a second too late—and caught the puck flush in his face. He was sidelined for several weeks with a damaged beak.

By 1955 the pattern for the perfect modern defenseman was set by Doug Harvey of the Montreal Canadiens. Extremely mobile, Harvey possessed a knack for controlling the pace of a game by his movements behind his own blue line. If Harvey decided that a speedy spurt was necessary, he would gallop from behind his net and race straight up the middle of the rink with his teammates on the fly. At other times Harvey believed it worthwhile to decrease the pace of the game. He would laconically dribble the puck in his defensive zone, defying the opposition to take it away. Then, when he believed that the time was right, Harvey would catapult to the attack, careful to pass the puck to a forward rather than trapping himself deep in enemy territory.

Hardly the robust type, Harvey was one of many compact defensemen who excelled, utilizing guile, as well as a well-timed stick check. A long time opponent of Harvey who adopted many of the Montreal defenseman's best moves was Pierre Pilote of the Chicago Black Hawks. A five-time First All-Star team member, Pilote almost seemed fragile as he skated alongside his mammoth partner, Elmer "Moose" Vasco. But Pilote, who won the Norris Trophy three times, was as mean and tough as a gila monster.

Defensive play style continued its change. Pilote, who was adept at body checking, would frequently charge up ice on daring rushes at the enemy goal.

Another speed merchant who excelled for the Detroit Red Wings was Marcel Pronovost. Marcel scored 345 points in 1,206 regular season games from 1950 through the 1969–70 season although his last two seasons produced poor results. During Stanley Cup play-off action he scored 31 points in 134 games. His Red Wings' sidekick, Red Kelly, also did considerable attacking. This technique stood Kelly in good stead when he later was traded to Toronto. Maple Leafs manager-coach Punch Imlach converted Kelly to a center and he also starred at his new position.

In the mid 1960s, when the hockey world began to learn that a prodigy named Robert Gordon "Bobby" Orr was tearing up the Ontario Junior A League, two defensemen dominated the NHL. Unlike Orr who is virtually obsessed with scoring, Harry Howell of the Rangers and the Canadiens' Jacques Laperriere maintained the posture of defensive defensemen. While they were not averse to scoring goals, they focused their attention on preventing the opposition from scoring. Laperriere won the Norris Trophy as the NHL's best defenseman in 1966. Howell won it a year later.

By that time Bobby Orr had graduated from amateur hockey to the big league and it was clear to everyone that the mode of defensive play never

124

Superstars such as Bobby Orr (No. 4) and Brad Park (No. 2) rarely come to grips with each other in battle. But the exception occasionally takes place when the game turns especially bitter.

The Rangers' Steve Vickers grimaces under the weight of St. Louis' defense-man Bob Gassoff, who has deactivated him in the Blues' crease. Goalie John Davidson follows the puck's flight at the other end of the pileup.

would be the same. Nobody realized that more than Harry Howell himself who had watched in awe as the wunderkind from Boston did more attacking than defending and, even more amazing, got away with it.

At the annual NHL awards banquet held in Montreal in June 1967, Howell told the audience as he clutched the Norris Trophy that he did not expect to win it again; nor did he expect anybody else to annex the trophy in the next decade but Orr.

Old-timers scoffed. After all, the NHL was loaded with superb defensemen such as Tim Horton, Ted Harris, J. C. Tremblay and of course, Howell and Laperriere.

"I realize that there are a lot of good men around," said Howell, "but there's never been one like Bobby Orr."

Howell, of course, was right. With his extraordinary repertoire of moves, Orr immediately took over as the game's most accomplished defenseman and its dominating personality. In June 1975 he won the Norris Trophy for the eighth consecutive time. Nobody since Howell has won the prize other than Bobby Orr.

Defensive Techniques

In pre-World War II hockey the defensemen were traditionally built along the generous dimensions of dromedaries. They were big, plodding types not especially known for their speed or stickhandling abilities. There were exceptions, to be sure, but for the most part defensemen were expected to defend and hit the enemy whenever possible. The modern defender is expected to attack as well as defend. The best of the contemporary blueliners—Bobby Orr, Denis Potvin, Brad Park—all are experts at the same stickhandling, shooting and play making techniques as forwards. In addition, the defenders are expected to body check as much as possible and keep the goal area free of intruders.

Several defending techniques are employed by today's defensemen. The traditional method of intercepting the puck is known as the poke check. It is executed while skating backwards. The defenseman, facing the attacker, holds his stick at the top of its shaft, keeping the stick blade on the ice as close as possible to his skates. When the attacker comes within striking distance, the defenseman thrusts his stick at the puck, like a striking cobra, and with a poke deflects it off the enemy's stick blade.

First cousin to the poke check is the sweep check. Instead of using a rapier-like thrust, the defender sweeps the blade of the stick in a circular motion along the ice, hoping to relieve the opponent of the rubber. Any number of variations on these stick movements are available to the defender.

More robust types like to use their bodies to dispatch the enemy to the ice and thereby gain control of the puck. The time-honored method is called the hip check. To execute this defensive maneuver, the backliner must perfectly synchronize his movements, otherwise he faces the embarrassment of a missed check. In working the hip check, the defender skates backwards as his opponent prepares to skate around either side. As the shooter makes his move the defender, in a half crouch, throws out his hip in such a way as to send the intercepted foe head over heels onto the ice.

Sometimes the defenseman's shoulder can be as useful in blocking the enemy as his hip. In delivering a shoulder check the defender again must time his movements exactly so as not to charge foolishly against thin air. If correctly implemented the shoulder check and hip check can devastate an unprepared shooter.

From time to time, a left defenseman and a right defenseman are able to coordinate their moves so accurately as to lure a misguided attacker into a human vise, otherwise known as the sandwich play. This takes place when an attacker tries to split two defenders who are side by side with a small opening between them. The defensemen try to lure the attackers to the opening, suggesting that it is wider than it actually is. When the shooter rushes for the opening the defenders close the gap and sandwich him in with their hips and/or shoulders.

Such a play was believed to be the maneuver that catapulted Minnesota North Stars' forward Bill Masterton to the ice in a game against the Oakland Seals in 1968. Masterton moved against the rugged defense pair of Larry Cahan and Ron Harris. The Oakland defensemen closed the vise and Masterton crashed to the ice. The blow proved fatal to Masterton, who died two days later.

Keeping the goal area free of intruders, a seemingly simple chore, is actually quite complicated. The defenseman is expected to move the enemy out of position and do so cleanly. However, a firmly planted foe often cannot be moved by a simple shoulder rub or a thrust of the hips. Usually, a combination of the two with a little stick push (not always legal) is employed.

The most trying moments for a defenseman occur when the opposition has a man advantage and generates a power play. With the aid of two penalty killing forwards the defensemen line up in box formation. The forwards are in tandem near the blue line and the defensemen are in tandem just outside the goal crease. Their objective is to keep the puck and the enemy shooters from entering the box and getting into scoring position.

Occasionally, defenders are called upon to act as second goaltenders. If a shooter winds up and telegraphs his drive a defender will hurl his body in the direction of the shot and attempt to block it before it reaches the goal. This is an extremely dangerous defensive maneuver, both physically and psychologically, but it is one frequently employed in various forms by the intrepid men who play defense.

Protecting the area in front of the goal—and his goalie—is a primary function of a defenseman. Few do it better than Denis Potvin of the New York Islanders. Goalie Glenn Resch stands ready as Potvin blocks Philadelphia Flyers' center Bobby Clarke, thus preventing Clarke from getting his stick free for a shot or deflection on goal. And cleanly, too.

Potential danger for players lurks in every hockey game. Barry Ashbee, once the best defenseman on the Philadelphia Flyers, lost the sight of an eye during a play-off game against the Rangers in 1974. Ashbee (left) is shown trying to stop the Rangers' Jean Ratelle in play at the goalmouth, prior to his injury. Ashbee was later named assistant coach of the Flyers.

Continuously atop the WHA, the New England Whalers' success is largely attributable to a solid defense headed by defenseman Brad Selwood (No. 3) and goalie Al Smith.

Gary Dornhoefer comes to the aid of a goalie in distress, Bernie Parent, as Flyers' defenseman Ed Van Impe looks on. Rick Martin of Buffalo is in no position to do anything about the loose puck.

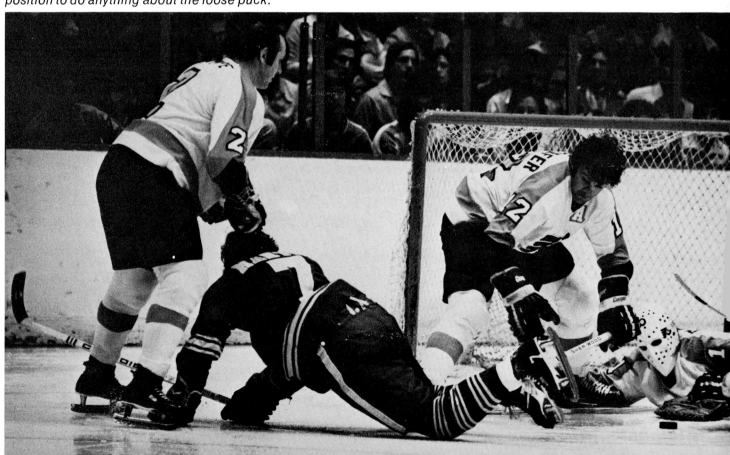

Peter Mahovlich, behemoth forward of the Montreal Canadiens, has emerged as the new leader of the Flying Frenchmen. Using his abundant physique to advantage Mahovlich is able to withstand body blows that would crumble smaller skaters.

The one-two punch of the Boston Bruins —Bobby Orr (No. 4) and Phil Esposito (No. 7). This defenseman-center combination has been one of the most productive in NHL history. In 1974-75 Orr finished first in scoring and Esposito was second. Frequently the two—they are close friends both on and off the ice—work special give-and-go plays. Orr will launch the attack in his own defensive zone, pass off to Esposito, and then sprint along the boards—or through center ice—and take a return pass accelerating as he rounds the enemy defenses. The play is often reversed with Esposito starting the attack, handing off to Orr and then receiving the headman pass. Each complements the other's style, both artistically and psychologically. Quiet and withdrawn, Orr often avoids interviews in the dressing room. In contrast, Esposito is gregarious and fun loving and frequently kids teammates and reporters alike.

The Front Lines— Forwards and Offense

In its earliest days professional hockey was a seven man game. A goaltender was flanked by two defensemen. The attacking formation included a center, a left wing and a right wing while the "rover" was the swing man, alternating between offense and defense as the need arose.

While the role of defenseman was altered from pure defense to a more offense oriented position, it is still the forwards who have the prime function— to score goals. As a rule, they have been the most exciting players in the rink and the names of the great ones—Howie Morenz, Maurice Richard, Bobby Hull, Gordie Howe—have always inspired pride and admiration in the hearts of hockey fans.

Some of the outstanding forwards appeared even more colorful because of their nicknames. Richard became "The Rocket." Morenz was "The Stratford Streak." Hull was named "The Golden Jet." But before any of these ice titans were born there was hockey's first major superstar, a human lightning bolt they called "Cyclone."

His real name was Fred Taylor and he developed his scoring eye while playing for the Listowel, Ontario, Junior club. Taylor first achieved eminence in the winter of 1904 in Toronto, where Listowel faced the Kingston Frontenacs for the Junior championship of Ontario. More than 600 Listowel fans came by train to Toronto to watch Taylor in action, and although their favorites lost to Kingston, Fred never let them down.

Those were the days when a hockey match was divided into halves. Listowel fell behind, 4–1, in the first half before Taylor got into high gear.

It was Fred Taylor—with the inadvertent aid of Captain James Sutherland who served as official timekeeper—who helped inspire the eventual use of time clocks in hockey. The Listowel ace scored three goals in succession to tie the score, 4–4, but two of the goals were scored after the first half had officially ended. The problem, as Captain Sutherland later informed the world at large, was that he was so hemmed in by spectators on both sides that it was impossible to get out of his seat to inform the referee that the first half had expired.

A few seconds after Taylor had scored his three goal "hat trick" Sutherland finally fought his way to the side of the rink, vaulted the boards and informed referee Pink Lillie that two of Taylor's goals were something less than legitimate. A high level conference was held with Lillie and John Ross Robertson, the president of the Ontario Hockey Association. In one of the first landmark decisions in hockey history the ice jurists ruled that the last two goals should count.

Racing for the puck usually provides a dramatic scene. Here, Christian Bordeleau, then with the St. Louis Blues, uses his body and his arm to thwart a pursuer.

Insight into hockey games is often provided by the players via the conduit of the press. Post-match interviews have become part of the warp and woof of hockey reporting. Here Vic Hadfield of the Pittsburgh Penguins holds court before a group of newsmen.

Garry Unger of the St. Louis Blues shoots the puck at the Chicago goal and goalie Tony Esposito prepares to stop it.

Thoughtful Rick MacLeish fixes his eyes on the face-off circle and the puck as he prepares to take the draw. One of the NHL's most gifted shooters and skaters, MacLeish relies on his brains as much as his brawn.

The play has gone the other way and the Buffalo Sabres' Rick Martin follows its trail.

Offensive hockey was paced differently in the early halcyon days of the sport. Rinks were never resurfaced between periods so that by the third period they were rutted and conducive to scrambly, sloppy hockey. Skates were not engineered as carefully nor designed for speed as today's models and the plays were slowed down by the fact that few teams carried substitutes. It was not uncommon for a player to skate 60 minutes of a match without a substitute.

In the twenties, hockey's popularity grew in the United States. The game, however, lacked one important ingredient: a goal-scorer who could be to hockey what Babe Ruth was to baseball, the equivalent of a real home run hitter. Then along came Howie Morenz. Morenz signed with the Montreal Canadiens as a rookie in the 1923–24 season and from then on real meaning was given to the club's nickname, "The Flying Frenchmen."

Raw speed was Howie's forte as he gained a varsity center ice berth on Les Canadiens. Within weeks he was dubbed "The Stratford Streak," "The Mitchell Meteor," and assorted other appellations that almost, but never quite, described his presence on the ice. "The kid's too *fast*," said one observer. "He'll burn himself out."

Morenz scored his first goal in the *bleu, blanc, et rouge* uniform of Les Canadiens against Ottawa on December 26, 1923, before 8,300 spectators at the spanking new Ottawa Auditorium, a curious looking egg-shaped rink. Ottawa's Senators dominated the NHL that season, thanks in part to a miniscule defenseman by the name of Francis "King" Clancy who would go on to become one of hockey's most delightful personalities as a referee, coach and vice-president of the Toronto Maple Leafs.

Clancy gave Morenz a once-over in practice and concluded there was nothing very special about him. "He was only an inch taller than I was," said Clancy. "That gave me the confidence I needed for starters."

Inevitably, Morenz captured the puck and launched a rush in Clancy's direction. King's linemate covered the other Canadiens' forward, enabling Clancy to get a dead bead on Howie, who, by this time, was under a full head of steam. King had sized up the situation as well as he could. Morenz was a left-handed shot; he figured to cut to

138

his left when he reached poke checking distance; everything perfectly calculated for King's riposte.

Morenz barreled right in on King and neither zigged nor zagged. He released a slap shot, skated right into Clancy and bowled him on his derriere. Howie didn't score on the play, but as he returned to center ice Clancy pulled himself together and warned the rookie, "One more run like that and I'll knock your block off."

The kid was singularly unimpressed. After digesting Clancy's warning, he replied that he planned to pull off the very same play as soon as he received the puck again. "Believe it or not," said the King, "he did *exactly* what he said he'd do."

Morenz scored thirteen goals in his rookie season to finish in a tie with Jack Adams for seventh place in scoring. He was well on his way to becoming the glamour boy of hockey, a man admired as much by his opponents as by his teammates and fans. Howie played the game as cleanly as was possible in those rambunctious days of chronic stick fights and butt ends.

One of the NHL's agile young forwards,
Jerry Butler, outraces Mike Bloom.

In a game at Madison Square Garden he knocked out four of Bun Cook's front teeth with the end of his stick as the pair was battling for the puck. Howie immediately dropped his stick and helped Bun off the ice.

Morenz was a superstar in his second year of big league play. He finished second in scoring to Cecil "Babe" Dye of Toronto and was doing things with the puck that astonished even such skeptics as Conn Smythe, founder of the Maple Leaf empire and the venerable dean of hockey in Toronto.

According to Smythe, Morenz executed "the most amazingly impossible play" he had ever seen in hockey up until that time. It was accomplished against the Boston Bruins who had a big, rugged team and had managed to ram Morenz forcefully into the boards on more than one occasion. Somehow, Morenz responded to the battering by skating even faster than he had before he was hit. Finally, Eddie Shore and Lionel Hitchman of the Boston defense prepared to sandwich Morenz between their powerful bodies as he tried to split the defense. Suddenly Howie leaped forward and crashed through like an auto speeding past two closing railroad gates at a crossing.

Just then a Bruin forward swerved in behind his defense to intercept Morenz. Seeing that he couldn't elude the checking wing, Howie released his shot from twenty-five feet in front of the net. The shot missed the goalpost by a few inches and caromed off the end boards right back to the blue line and onto Shore's waiting stick.

The Bruin defenseman, one of the speediest rushers hockey has ever known, orbited into a breakaway with all the Montreal players caught in Bruin territory along with Morenz.

"I was watching Howie all the time," said Smythe later, "and I saw him follow up his shot with a long leap in preparation to circling the net. To this day I can't figure out how he managed to stay on his skates as he rounded the cage."

Meanwhile, Shore was away at top speed for the Canadiens' goal. Nobody in the rink, let alone Smythe, doubted that the Bruin would have plenty of time for an easy play on goal and a likely score. That is, all but Morenz. He had put his head down and dashed in pursuit of Shore.

Shore was about to enter the final stages of his maneuvering when Morenz suddenly cut directly *in front* of him, released the puck from the Boston player's blade, and immediately changed direction for another play on the Bruin goal. "Shore," said Smythe, "was absolutely dumbfounded. As for me, I actually was unable to move my mouth, I was so awed by the play. Morenz had done what he was to do for years to come—he took my breath away!"

Many respected hockey observers claim that Morenz was singly responsible for the successful expansion of the NHL into the United States in the 1920s. New York sports promoter Tex Rickard became a hockey fan the moment he spied Morenz in action and not long afterward Rickard introduced the Rangers to New York.

Morenz's competitive spirit was matched by only one other member of Les Canadiens, Maurice Richard, in the 1940s and 1950s. But in the twenties, the fires of competition burned fiercely in the heart of Morenz.

One time in Boston, Morenz was unable to sleep because he felt he had not done his best. The play that so disturbed Howie was a face-off he had lost to Cooney Weiland of the Bruins. A split second

Bobby Clarke dribbles the puck along the corner boards en route to a foray in enemy territory.

after the referee had dropped the puck it flew into the air. Weiland batted it down with his hand and promptly shot it into the net in the same motion. The goal won the game for the Bruins.

Eight hours later a sobbing Howie was still blaming himself for the goal as he slumped into a chair in Montreal newsman Elmer Ferguson's hotel room.

"He buried his face in his hands," wrote Ferguson. "His shoulders shook because he was crying like a little boy. He was heartbroken. He felt that he alone was responsible for the defeat . . . In all the history of hockey there never was a more sincere competitor."

A Morenz ritual was to arrive at the dressing room at least an hour before game time. "He'd restlessly pace around the long promenade," Ferguson recalled, "as high-strung as a thoroughbred that is being readied for a race."

It was easy enough for Montreal players and writers to wax ecstatic about Morenz and it was not uncommon for opponents to do likewise. But when the opponent happened to be Eddie Shore, the fiercest defenseman in the game, *then* Morenz knew he had arrived.

"He's the hardest player in the league to stop," Shore admitted. "Howie comes at you with such speed that it's almost impossible to block him with a body check. When he hits you he usually comes off a lot better than the defenseman. Another thing that bothers us is his shift. He has a knack of swerving at the last minute that can completely fool you. Everybody likes Howie. He's one player who doesn't deserve any rough treatment."

By the time Morenz was thirty-three years old he had obviously slowed down to a point where he could be more easily stopped by the opposition. Just prior to the 1934–35 season Dandurand dropped a bombshell—Howie Morenz had been traded to the Chicago Black Hawks.

After eleven years with the Canadiens, the most popular Montreal hockey player since Georges Vezina was being cast adrift. Even so, in honor of his friend, Dandurand tossed a farewell dinner for Morenz and told the audience, "As long as I'm associated with the Canadiens, no other player will wear Howie's number seven."

Proof that a small man can excel in the big league hockey jungle. The Chicago Black Hawks' center Pit Martin has been among the NHL's leading scorers for nearly a decade.

The Toronto Maple Leafs have been accenting more and more of the speedy young hockey players such as high scoring forward Darryl Sittler.

Dandurand's promise has been kept by his successors. To this day no other player has carried number seven.

Although admittedly unhappy in Chicago, Howie played a scintillating game for the Black Hawks and scored against his old teammates in the final game of the season at the Forum in which Chicago triumphed, 4–2. Howie received a standing ovation from the Montreal crowd.

A season later Morenz was dealt to the Rangers, but he was a shadow of his former self and New York's Lester Patrick was happy to return him to Les Canadiens for the 1936–37 season.

Wearing the *bleu, blanc, et rouge* once more proved to be a tonic for Morenz. True, he had lost his old getaway power, but every so often he'd bring the Forum crowd to its feet as he executed one of the exquisite Morenz rushes.

He was doing just that on the night of January 28, 1937, at the Forum when a Chicago defenseman caught him with a body check, sending Morenz hurtling feet first into the end boards. It wasn't a normal spill and Howie lost all control as he

Guy Lafleur whose stickhandling has a magical quality wore a helmet during his early days with the Montreal Canadiens. He eschewed the headpiece during the 1974-75 season and enjoyed the most bountiful scoring period of his career.

141

skidded toward the boards. As his skate rammed into the wood, a sharp report was heard and Morenz crumpled in excruciating pain.

Howie was rushed to the hospital, his leg badly broken. In the hospital the thirty-six year old Morenz began brooding about his fate. Instead of recuperating, he suffered a nervous breakdown. Then he developed heart trouble.

Nobody is quite sure what transpired to cause Howie's utter deterioration. Early on March 8, 1937, Morenz was given a complete checkup. It appeared he was rallying. It was an inaccurate prognosis. A few hours later Howie Morenz was dead.

Although many first-rate forwards such as Syl Apps, Milt Schmidt, Bill Cowley and Bryan Hextall gained acclaim as stars after Morenz's death, none made the imprint on big league hockey the way Maurice "Rocket" Richard did in the mid-forties. A native of Montreal, Richard made his debut with the Canadiens in the 1942–43 season and scored his first NHL goal on November 8, 1942. Playing in his third NHL game in the Forum, against the New York Rangers, Richard made a pulsating end to end rush through the Ranger defense like a pinball bouncing its way past obstacles to its goal. Richard's shot beat Ranger goalie Steve Buzinski, and a superstar was born.

More than anyone it was short-tempered, vitriolic Canadiens' coach Dick Irvin who convinced Richard he would become a star.

Irvin had decided that Elmer Lach was the ideal center for Richard but he wasn't sure about left wing. He finally decided that Toe Blake would be worthy and in no time the line was made—for keeps. The trio, soon to be named "the Punch Line," finished one-two-three (Lach, Blake, Richard) in scoring on the team, with Richard collecting 32 goals and 22 assists for 54 points in 46 games.

In his first full season in the NHL, Richard set two big records. One was for scoring five goals in a single game (against Toronto in the Stanley Cup play-off) and another for amassing 12 goals in the play-off series (three against Chicago in one game). Les Canadiens were soon quaffing champagne from the Stanley Cup.

142

Oddly enough the reaction to Richard's accomplishments was not totally enthusiastic. "He won't last," was a familiar cry whenever Richard was discussed. "Let's see what he'll do *next* year," was another.

When the next year arrived, Les Canadiens iced virtually the same team they had when they won the Stanley Cup with a few exceptions. The Punch Line remained intact and launched the season with the same syncopated attack that had stirred the fans in 1943–44. Richard seemed particularly bolstered by a full season under his belt without serious injury and he broke from the post like an overzealous thoroughbred. His scoring became so prolific that opposing coaches began mapping specific strategies to stop Maurice alone, on the theory that if you could block Richard you could beat Les Canadiens.

With four games remaining in the season, Les Canadiens, snug in first place, invaded Madison Square Garden and routed the Rangers 11–5. Banging two shots past goalie Ken McAuley, Richard lifted his goal scoring mark to an astonishing 48 in only 47 games.

The Rocket scored number 49 on March 15, 1945, with only two games remaining on the schedule. In the next to last game, against the Black Hawks on Forum ice, Les Canadiens triumphed, but somehow Maurice was thoroughly blanked. That left only one more match, the final game of the season at Boston Garden. This time Richard came through in a 4–2 win over the Bruins and he finished the season with 50 goals in 50 games, a modern hockey record that has never been and will likely never be equalled.

Richard's accomplishment automatically equated him with the mightiest baseball slugger of all, Babe Ruth. Big goals were soon described around the NHL as "Richardian" in their epic quality and, year after year, Richard seemed to outdo himself in producing thrills until his retirement from the Canadiens in 1960.

The torch, by then, had been passed to his younger brother, Henri. Less robust than Maurice, but a speedier skater, Henri "The Pocket Rocket" further glorified the Richard name and the Canadiens remained the dominant offensive team in 143 hockey—The Flying Frenchmen—throughout his reign in the sixties and early seventies.

While Henri Richard was a throwback to the old-line hockey scorers epitomized by his brother Maurice, a flock of new and exciting skaters made their imprint on the sport in the 1960s and 1970s.

If Rocket Richard had been hockey's Babe Ruth in scoring, Bobby Hull became the Mickey Mantle of the ice. Muscular, good looking and possessing extraordinary strength, Hull made his mark as the Golden Jet of the Chicago Black Hawks. His dynamic slap shot and overpowering rink length dashes brought a new and exciting dimension to the game. Hull's sidekick on the Black Hawks, Stan Mikita developed into a stickhandler of many maneuvers that resembled the style of Gordie Howe.

Hull was not the only successful practitioner of the slap shot. Andy Bathgate of the New York Rangers shot the puck so hard one night that he nearly killed Montreal goalie Jacques Plante. That experience caused Plante to adopt a face mask, soon to become standard equipment throughout the league.

Among the more gifted smaller forwards was little Dave Keon who made up in speed what he lacked in muscle. His Toronto Maple Leaf sidekick, George Armstrong, was a plodding skater who compensated for this deficiency by tenacious checking and abundant puck savvy. Armstrong was inducted into the Hockey Hall of Fame in 1975.

When the NHL expanded in 1967 to twelve teams, another type of superstar came to the game. This was the player who had been, because of oversight or petty prejudice, buried in the minors or on the bench of an NHL team. Typical of this genre was Gordon "Red" Berenson who had been virtually dismissed by the Montreal Canadiens and New York Rangers but achieved super-stardom with the St. Louis Blues. One night Berenson scored six goals against the Philadelphia Flyers in a regular season NHL game.

Expansion also meant more opportunities for young players, among them a young, speedy French Canadian, Marcel Dionne, who won the Lady Byng Trophy in 1975. The Buffalo Sabres produced one of the most spectacular front line trios of the 1970s with the French Connection featuring Gil Perreault, Rene Robert and Richard Martin.

The Montreal Canadiens were not without Gallic offensive aces. Yvan Cournoyer exhibited such electric speed he became known as "The Road-runner," Guy Lafleur had all of the stickhandling, shooting and play making qualities of an earlier Montreal Hall of Famer, Jean Beliveau.

No forward from the turn of the century to the start of the 1970s exhibited more perseverance and grim determination than Bobby Clarke, captain of the Philadelphia Flyers, and one of the most gifted and inspirational leaders in sports. His sidekick, Rick MacLeish, has all the clutch scoring qualities of Rocket Richard and he has "rediscovered" the effective wrist shot.

By 1975 the galaxy of offensive superstars was never brighter. Stickhandlers such as Pete Mahovlich, Phil Esposito, Rod Gilbert, Steve Vickers, Tom Lysiak, Eric Vail and Garry Unger proved that hockey more than ever was an offensive game and that nothing was more dazzling nor exciting than the art of putting the puck in the net.

Right: *The hockey rink is marked in a number of different ways. There are five face-off circles and eight red face-off dots. There are two blue lines and a center dotted red line that cross the rink laterally. At each end of the rink are two goals, each with a goal crease. And at the end of the rink are two additional red lines which are used to determine offside. In addition, there is a semi-circle at the side of the rink, next to the boards.*

The game, and each of the two other periods (hockey is the only sport with three segments of play) begin with the puck being dropped at the center face-off circle. At other times when play is stopped the face-off circles and dots are used to resume play. (Actually, face-offs may be held in other parts of the rink.) Play is stopped for any number of reasons such as a penalty being called, offside, an injury to a player, etc.

The blue lines and the center red line divide the ice into zones. The center line is dotted to help television viewers with black and white sets distinguish between the red and blue lines.

The lines which jut out from the face-off circles indicate the area into which opposing players may not cross.

The small semicircle (bottom) is the place to which the referee retreats when he calls a penalty. A player may not enter this area without also being subject to a penalty.

On the Attack

Left: *Over the blue line; the Detroit Red Wings expertly execute a traditional attack. The play began when Gordie Howe (upper right) passed the puck at center ice to defenseman Bill Gadsby (No. 4). In possession of the puck, Gadsby then skimmed the pass to Parker MacDonald (No. 14) who was on the right side of the line—therefore, on side when he received the pass. MacDonald then sped over the line into the attacking zone. Had the pass come later, and MacDonald had been on the left side of the blue line, the play would have been whistled down for an offside.*

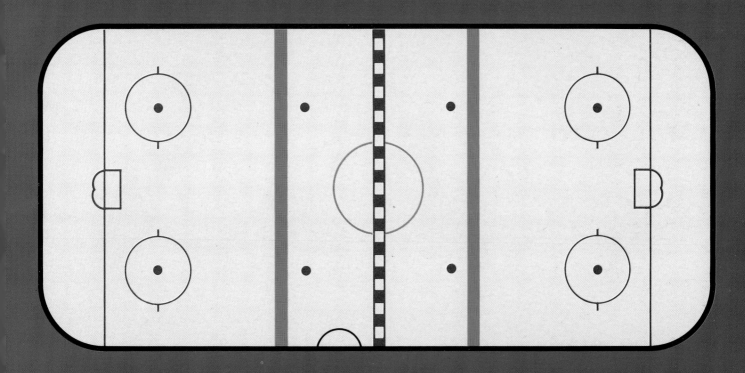

Jockeying for position: Superstars, centers Bobby Clarke of the Philadelphia Flyers and Phil Esposito of the Boston Bruins, struggle for free space in front of the Bruins' net. Esposito, his right skate firmly dug into the ice for leverage, attempts to keep his torso between his team's goalie, Gilles Gilbert, and the attacker. Clarke struggles to free his stick so that he will be able to deflect a centering pass into the net.

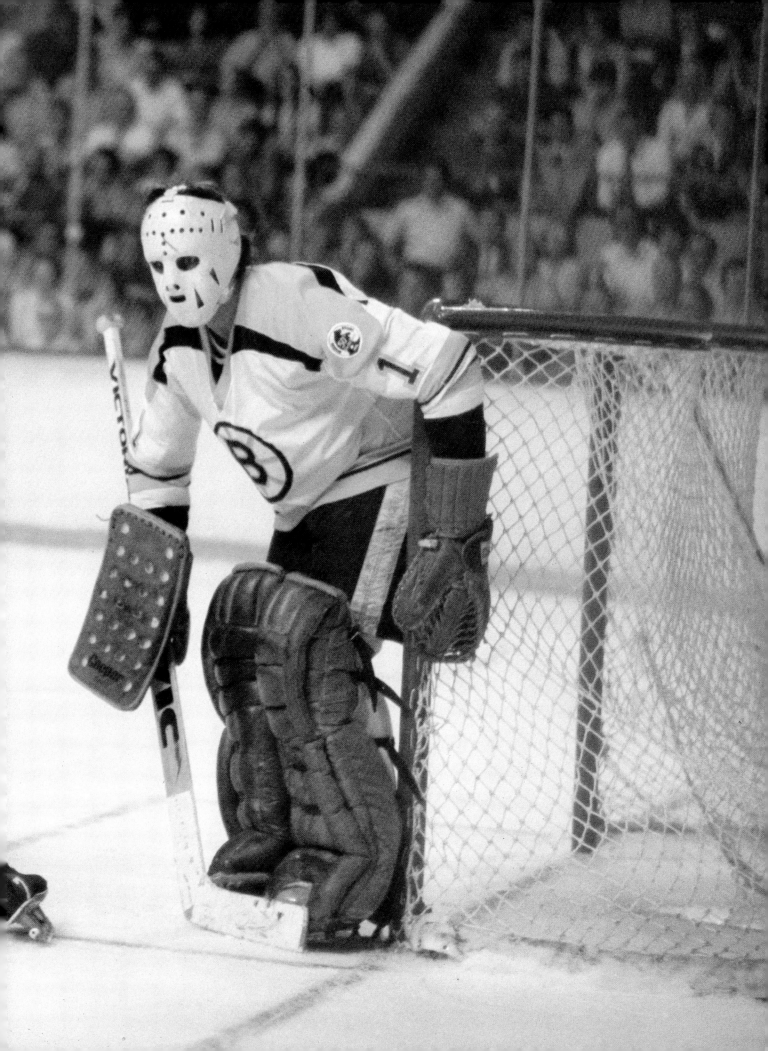

Ron Ellis strikes mightily at the puck, demonstrating an outstanding example of the slap shot, that still controversial hockey stroke. The slap shot was originated in the 1950's by Bernie ''Boom Boom'' Geoffrion, then of the Montreal Canadiens. It is delivered by drawing the stick back as far behind and over the head as one can go, much in the manner one would with a golf club, then swinging at the puck which is often in full flight, striking it as a golfer would hit a powerful drive.

The Remarkable Howe Family: *Of all the hockey families the Howes are most likely to be the longest remembered. Gordie Howe played professional hockey for 28 years, 25 of them with the Detroit Red Wings from 1946 to 1971. Following a two year hiatus during which he chafed at routine administrative and public relations chores, he once again returned to the ice with the Houston Aeros of the World Hockey Association. In 1975, at the age of 47, he retired from active playing. During the two years he was with the Aeros he had the pleasure of playing with his sons, Marty and Mark. Here, below, the Howes are lined up with other members of the Aeros shaking hands with the San Diego Mariners whom they defeated in the semifinals of the WHA playoffs in May 1975. Reading from left to right the Howes are Mark (No. 4), Gordie (No. 9) with A (for alternate captain) on his shoulder and Marty (No. 3).*

The old master, Gordie Howe, demonstrates his power skating and mighty shooting against the Soviet National Hockey Team.

Above: He shoots! He scores!! The puck flies past goalie
Ken Dryden of the Montreal Canadiens in a contest
between the Buffalo Sabres and Montreal. Center Don
Luce, outside camera range, has fired the puck at the
goal. The score is celebrated by Buffalo forward Danny
Gare while goalie Dryden stares helplessly behind him
into the net.

Left: Poetry in motion. Los Angeles Kings' forward Butch Goring leans toward the ice as he crosses his right skate over his left in a speeding turn ready to launch a play up the ice.

Ron Ellis of the Toronto Maple Leafs flies gracefully through the air after having been tripped.

The Flyers' Bobby Clarke, one of the most agile skaters in professional hockey, demonstrates a counterattacking turn. His eyes focused on the defense ahead, Clarke brings his right leg over his left as he almost magically controls the puck at the base of his stick. As he skates he determines whether to pass to a teammate or attempt to plunge against the enemy defenses by himself.

Tommy Williams has played for Stanley Cup champions as well as losers; most recently for the Washington Capitals— one of the newest franchises on the NHL scene whose first year, the 1974-75 season, was disastrous.

One of the most difficult yet effective plays in hockey is performed when an offensive player sweeps around the net from behind it and catches the goaltender by surprise, whipping the puck between his pads into the opening— almost like threading a needle. Forward Bob Nystrom (right) of the New York Islanders gives a perfect demonstration of this play against Pittsburgh Penguins' goalie Gary Inness, while Islanders' teammate Andre St. Laurent moves in for the potential rebound.

Below: ANATOMY OF A GOAL. Goalie Gerry Desjardins of the Buffalo Sabres has been drawn from his net by a potential Philadelphia shot on goal. Ross Lonsberry (18), the puck handler, circles the fallen netminder. Confronted with a difficult angle at which to shoot, Lonsberry has the option to move behind the net and come out the other side. However, he chose to gamble with the difficult shot and managed to deposit the rubber into the right side of the cage for a goal. Sabres' defenseman Larry Carriere arrives on the scene too late and goalie Desjardins makes a futile attempt to return to the crease.

Above: Danny Gare of the Buffalo Sabres pushes the puck ahead, retaining careful control in a spurt at center ice while teammate Rick Martin prepares to move into passing position during the Sabres' power play.

Bottom Right: *International Play.* Members of the American National Hockey team scramble for the puck in front of the net guarded by the goalie representing the Soviet Union during an exhibition match at Madison Square Garden.

Left: *She doesn't look like a hockey player and she doesn't act like a hockey player but vocalist Kate Smith has been part of the Philadelphia Flyers' mystique. When Kate sings before a Flyers game—either in person or on a record—the odds are that Philadelphia is going to win. Miss Smith was on the ice prior to the seventh and final game of the 1975 Islanders–Flyers series at the Spectrum in Philadelphia. Needless to say the Flyers won the decisive game and marched headlong to the Cup with many thanks to Miss Kate.*

Two-thirds of the French Connection, Rene Robert (No. 14) and Richard Martin (No. 7).

A star on Broadway for more than a decade, Rod Gilbert (No. 7) of the New York Rangers wheels past the side of the Detroit Red Wings' net while awaiting a teammate's shot on goal.

Buffalo's Richard Martin during a break.

An enigma to many, Philadelphia Flyers' coach Fred Shero was the catalyst for two consecutive Stanley Cup championships. Wearing a Fu-Manchu mustache and his trademark, tinted glasses, Shero studies the play on the ice while his charges watch from the bench.

Once ridiculed as having no talent for the nuances of defensive play, Andre Dupont (right) found a haven in Philadelphia under coach Fred Shero. Dupont, who can body check with the best and shoot as powerfully as most high scoring forwards, moves away from New York Islanders' captain Ed Westfall during the 1975 Stanley Cup play-offs.

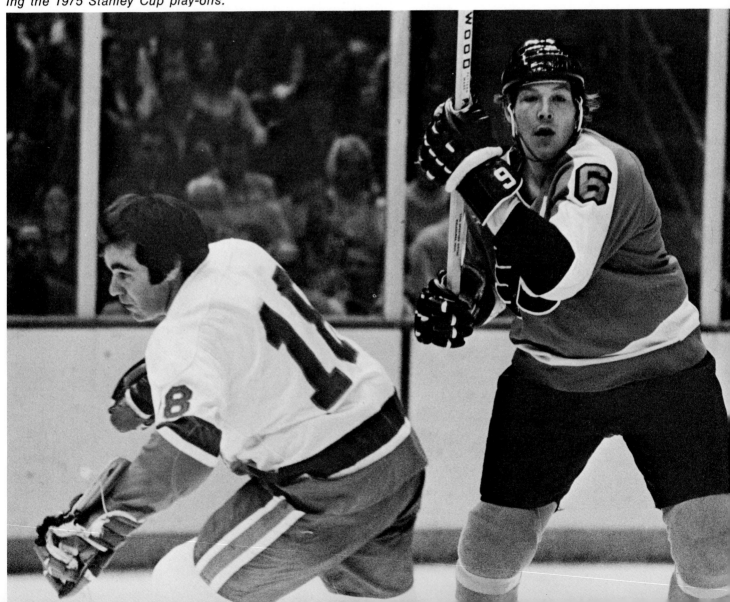

Hockey's Brain Trust-The Coaches

In the moments following the 1975 Stanley Cup play-off round in which the expansion team, Buffalo's Sabres, upset big league hockey's oldest club, the Montreal Canadiens, winner of more Stanley Cups than any other team, losing coach Scotty Bowman reflected on the revolutionary events that were indicative of current NHL play.

"We have to face the fact," said Bowman, "that hockey is changing radically."

And so it was.

In 1975 for the first time two expansion teams, Buffalo and Philadelphia, competed in the Stanley Cup finals. They were there not only because of the quality of their stickhandlers and scorers but also because of their brain trust—the coaches. Fred Shero of the Flyers and Floyd Smith of the Sabres represent hockey's new breed of coaches, the super-strategists.

In the past strategy was an aspect of hockey that was not given much attention. It was taken for granted when the NHL was a six-team league in 1966 that you sent five skaters onto the ice and they would intuitively know what to do. The Canadiens epitomized that style.

They had aces such as Jean Beliveau, Henri Richard, Yvan Cournoyer, Jacques Lemaire and Ted Harris. They skated furiously from end to end in a manner that led one observer to describe it as "fire-wagon hockey." But Harris, who played for the Canadiens under Cup winning coach Toe Blake and for the Flyers under Cup winning coach Fred Shero, indicates that there was no method to their championships.

"Sometimes," says Harris, "three of our players would be in one corner chasing the puck which any coach will tell you is fundamentally bad hockey. But we had so much talent we could violate basic rules and still win. When someone like Beliveau took the puck across the blue line, it was beautiful to watch, like poetry in motion."

The change in thinking about hockey strategy took place with the arrival of Shero in Philadelphia. A thinking man's coach, Shero analyzed the teams with the biggest stars, Montreal and Boston at that time, and dogmatically asserted that he could beat them. The Canadiens still had the cream of the crop in Peter Mahovlich, Serge Savard, Jacques Lemaire, Yvan Cournoyer and Guy Lafleur. Boston boasted Bobby Orr and Phil Esposito, supposedly the best one-two punch in the game.

But the revolutionary thinking Shero insisted that Orr, despite all his points (he led the NHL in scoring in 1974–75) was lacking in teamwork because he monopolized the puck. "It destroys me," said Shero, "when I see someone like Orr having the puck all night. Is this a team game? Or is this golf or tennis? Orr is a great player, sure, but you've got to get players to use their talents for the good of everyone. You've got to get them to fit into a pattern. Of course, some teams don't have a pattern, but that's their fault."

Not only was there an absence of patterns, but few coaches stressed conditioning and still fewer employed sophisticated techniques such as a review of videotapes of previous games. When his Canadiens were eliminated from the 1975 play-offs, coach Bowman finally saw the light at the end of the coaching tunnel.

"There's a move," Bowman acknowledged, "toward the more systematic playing of hockey. There are going to be big inroads made from watching game films. That type of teaching method is going to be a big factor in the future. Conditioning also is going to be a very big factor in the near future. And more teams are going to look to Europe for their talent."

The need for a systematic approach to coaching was brought about by expansion. Newer teams such as Philadelphia were egregiously lacking in superstars. How, then, could they win against the talent laden older clubs? The answer, in Shero's estimation, was in discipline and self-sacrifice.

"To win against good competition," said Shero, "you have to set up two-on-one plays or three-on-ones, which is what our team does. It probably wouldn't work in Montreal because the players want to put the puck in the net themselves. Talent wise our Philadelphia team couldn't compare with Montreal. But we beat them because Montreal relies on one individual to have a super game or make the super play. With them everything is one-on-one."

It was not easy for the Canadiens to adopt a system. Old theories die slowly, especially in a game such as hockey which has always followed conservative thinking. "The inability to implement a proper system bothered me," Bowman stated. "We had played a system of sorts, but it wasn't a total system for 60 minutes.

"It has been proven in hockey today that if you can put the puck in the other team's end and fore-check them, that team is going to be in difficulty. Even guys like Bobby Orr can be contained because hockey is becoming full of big men who can skate.

"I can remember when I was in St. Louis [1967, 1968, 1969] we'd send just one guy in and the wingers would peel back. You can't do that anymore. The ability to fore-check is very important. The Philadelphia Flyers have proven that."

The Philadelphia system as preached by Shero is an offshoot of techniques developed by the former Soviet National Hockey Team coach Anatoli Tarasov. The Russians advocated team play—the same as in soccer—in which pattern passing plays

a major part, rather than the individual effort as epitomized by Bobby Orr. But Shero departed from the Tarasov technique when it came to body play, e.g., violence. European hockey traditionally has accented ballet over bloodshed. But in the NHL a team has to literally fight for every inch of ice.

"There are four corners to a rink," says Shero, "although a lot of players don't realize it. And there are two pits, one in front of each net. To win a game, you've got to win the corners and the pits. You give punishment there, and you take it, which is why we [the Flyers] have more fights than most teams."

Not having been blessed with puck carrying defensemen with the skills of Bobby Orr, Shero again borrowed from the Russians. The Flyers' defenders did not have to skate the puck to the enemy blue line; all they had to do was pass the puck to a waiting forward and then advance with the play at an appropriate and well specified distance.

"Once we are on the move with the puck," Shero explains, "no defenseman can be more than one zone—or two stick lengths—behind the puck carrier. In other words, once Bobby Clarke gets to center ice, I want a defenseman at the blue line. When Clarke reaches the far blue line, I want the defenseman at the red line. Once Clarke is ten feet inside the zone, the defenseman must be stationed at the point."

Although Shero has been most discussed in terms of the revolution in hockey coaching, there are other coaches who have contributed to the cerebral style. In Los Angeles Bob Pulford of the Kings, one of the few professional hockey coaches with both a B.A. and an M.A. degree, has done almost everything Shero has done except win a Stanley Cup. His defensemen, unlike Orr, remain back on defense. His passing style, as one observer noted, "resembles a game of connect-the-dots—short yet consistent progressions up ice."

Like Shero and other avant-garde coaches, Pulford places an extraordinary emphasis on psychology. "These days," says Pulford, "you take a school kid and tell him to go through the front door and he'll say, 'Why, the side door is closer.' I can't say, 'You have to wear a shirt and tie, you have to stay away from the hotel bar.' The players

Eager to get into the action, Philadelphia forward Ross Lonsberry leans over the boards awaiting his cue from coach Fred Shero.

ask questions. They have to understand your *purpose.*"

In the Pulford system, efficiency is more important than dramatic effect. "As a coach," he says, "I try to go to the basic intellect of a player. I don't believe there is such a thing as a miracle worker. It's the mind. Without the right mental outlook a player is not in the best physical condition. With previous coaches in Los Angeles the attitude of the team was, 'Well, we lost and that's that. So what?' We accepted losing. Now we react to a loss."

Pulford's college degrees may or may not enhance his coaching ability. The issue is debatable. What is certain is the fact that the best of the new breed of coaches are not necessarily college men. Al Arbour, who orchestrated the New York Islanders' climb from obscurity to fame in 1975, was described by spare defenseman Neil Nicholson as "a genius, and we all believe in him." Yet Arbour is not a college man.

Like Pulford and Shero, Arbour accents defensive as much as offensive hockey. And like his successful colleagues, Arbour emphasizes thought. He allows each player to coach the team at least once during practice, urging them to come up with different ideas to avoid the monotony of an 80-game season.

He gets his players to think about the games by having them give him written critiques on each team they face—line by line and player by player. He keeps the critiques in his desk drawer and studies them from time to time so that he can keep his own knowledge current as well.

There is an Arbour system just as there is a Shero system. Players are asked over and over to diagram plays that are used in particular situations. They are constantly reminded of their responsibilities if they have to switch lines.

Jean Potvin, the defenseman, played for both Shero and Arbour. Both, according to Potvin, have studied every facet of hockey to the nth degree. "They study the films of every game in detail," says Potvin, "and they're great with psychology. Freddie used to tell us, 'Dammit, you'd better go out and have a few beers tonight.' Al will come back on the bus with us and drink a few beers with the guys. The subject of beers wouldn't even come up with a lot of other coaches."

A journeyman forward during his NHL days, Floyd Smith has proven that some of the best coaches are those who never basked in the big league limelight. In his first year directing the Buffalo Sabres, Smith not only guided them into first place in their division, but also led them to the Stanley Cup finals.

168

The thinking man's coach is becoming more and more evident in the NHL these days. Los Angeles Kings' mentor Bob Pulford holds a B.A. and M.A. degree. His effectiveness as a hockey coach was underlined during the 1974-75 season when he propelled the Kings into a play-off berth.

Running a hockey team can be one of the most ulcer producing jobs in pro sports. Jack Gordon forsook the Minnesota North Stars' coaching job in the middle of the 1974-75 season although he remains as general manager.

One of the most difficult coaching jobs fell to Armand "Bep" Guidolin, who was asked to take the just born Kansas City Scouts and develop them into a club competitive with the established teams. Guidolin, who enjoys shouting behind the bench, did a creditable job with Kansas City in 1974-75.

Al Arbour, once an unheralded NHL defenseman who played for the Maple Leafs, the Black Hawks and the St. Louis Blues, was thrust into the limelight when as coach of the New York Islanders he led them to a startling comeback in the 1975 Stanley Cup play-offs against the Pittsburgh Penguins.

Quite often, the best judge of a coach is a player who has worked under that particular mentor. But few skaters have the opportunity to play for more than a handful of coaches. Those who have, such as utility forward Glen Sather, are in an excellent position to make insightful appraisals. Sather played for Harry Sinden, who coached the Stanley Cup winning Boston Bruins in 1970. He also skated for Emile Francis whose coaching win percentage is second only to Montreal's Toe Blake. In addition Sather played for Scotty Bowman, another Cup winning instructor, as well as for Red Kelly and Lou Angotti.

"Bowman," says Sather, "is a pretty good psychologist. He'll come into the dressing room and give guys hell for seemingly no reason at all—just to get them mad at him. What he really does is get the guys worked up. They really get sore at him . . . and he gets 'em going. Sometimes, though, he might pick on the wrong guy, and the guy just buries his head and sulks a little bit."

Francis, who doubled as the Rangers' general manager, relinquished the coaching job in New York three times, yet returned because of the failure of his choices (Red Sullivan, Larry Popein, Bernie Geoffrion). When Ron Stewart was named Rangers' coach in May 1975 he said that his former mentor (Francis) had one flaw: he was too good to his players. Sather echoed the thoughts:

"Emile never really picked on you. He'd never criticize you in front of anybody. Very seldom. If he was going to criticize you, he'd criticize the whole group and then you'd know he was criticizing you because he'd say something like, 'Well, the left-wingers against such and such a line aren't really doing the job.' And you'd know he was talking to you, but he wouldn't single you out and say, 'Well, Sather, you played badly tonight.' He'd never do that. I like a guy who treats you like a gentleman, and you don't have to worry about him embarrassing you. But if you had it coming, you knew you'd get it from him."

By contrast Lou Angotti used a different and less successful approach according to Sather, when Angotti briefly coached the St. Louis Blues. "Angotti tried to create the atmosphere that he was going to be a Little Caesar. A guy would make a mistake and he'd yell at you right away. You don't do anything like that.

What does a hockey coach do during a game? He changes lines, plans overall strategy, and frequently screams at referees. Emile Francis, manager of the New York Rangers since 1964 and often its coach as well, demonstrates the art of high decibel protestation.

"Red Kelly did that, too. He'd jump on guys right away. But all that does is take away a guy's confidence. If a guy makes a mistake, you should pat him on the back and say, 'Well, you should have done this or you should have done that.' You shouldn't say, 'You s.o.b., you're stupid.'"

Sinden proved one of the more controversial coaches when he led Team Canada 1972 to a triumph over the Soviet National team in an eight game exhibition series. No fewer than four players walked out in protest against Sinden on the grounds that they were being ignored by the coach. However, Sather commends Sinden. "He'd pick you out and tell you you weren't playing well. He'd say, 'You gotta get going.' But he wouldn't accuse you of having a night on the town, or whatever."

The ability to rally a team from the depths of despair is a gift possessed by few coaches. When the Flyers blew a three game lead to the Islanders in 1975 and faced possible humiliation in front of the home crowd in the seventh game at the Spectrum, Shero was advised to spend the night before the climactic game in seclusion with his players. But he rejected the idea as stupid.

"Montreal always hides in the mountains," said Shero. "Before big games all the players ever do is stare at each other. What good is that? Why run away from people? I'd rather take them into the heart of traffic, let them see the girls and relax."

One of the most perplexing matters for big league hockey coaches involves loyalty to players. Some believe in a thoroughly detached approach while others such as Francis have been loyal to a fault.

"The only thing I found wrong with Francis," said Sather, "was that maybe he was too loyal to some guys. By that I mean if a player was a superstar, Emile wouldn't sit him down even if he was having a lousy game. Some nights Brad Park just didn't have it. If it had happened to somebody else, he'd be on the bench. But Emile wouldn't do it to Brad because he was a superstar and played well most of the time.

"That's where Francis and Bowman are different. I think Scotty would bench his mother if he

Rangers' boss Emile Francis (behind bench) seems to be reflecting on other aspects of the game as Islanders' captain Ed Westfall charges past Rod Gilbert. Gilbert's stick is upraised in a typical reflex motion of defense after a collision.

thought she wasn't playing well. I don't think Scotty gives a damn whether or not a player is a fan favorite or a superstar, or whatever, I don't think he worries about that at all. I think his only concern is winning."

To produce a winner, coaches and managers employ every available technique nowadays from the aforementioned films and TV tapes to the hoariest bromides. A slogan in the Toronto Maple Leafs' dressing room reads: "Defeat Does Not Rest Lightly On Our Shoulders." The Rangers posted a slogan: "We Supply Everything But Guts." At the Forum in Montreal, the Canadiens emblazoned a passage from Dr. John MacCrae's famous war poem, "In Flanders Field," "To you we pass the torch . . ."

Fred Shero's office is enriched by a sign that reads: "O, the despair of Pygmalion, who might have created a statue and only made a woman."

For variety of inspiration, Shero keeps a blackboard in the Flyers' dressing room on which he chalks and then erases such aphorisms as:

Only he deserves power who every day justifies it.—Dag Hammarskjöld.

The messages have worked for Shero and so has his system. Up to a point. Punch Imlach won four Stanley Cup championships with the Toronto Maple Leafs but eventually was fired because, some critics claimed, he couldn't relate to his players. Then, Imlach moved to Buffalo, took an expansion team and built it into a Stanley Cup finalist in the space of only five years.

Many critics regard Imlach as a hockey genius of the highest order. They praised him especially after his club wiped out the once proud Canadiens following two big score humiliating defeats of the Sabres at the hands of the Montreal team. Imlach's club rebounded like seasoned champions.

"That doesn't make me smarter than anybody else," Imlach concluded in as precise an analysis of his business as possible, "but it makes me luckier."

Bob "Battleship" Kelly releases a wrist shot against the New York Islanders as All-Star defenseman Denis Potvin belatedly stabs his stick at the puck with an attempted poke check.

Rick Martin of the Buffalo Sabres, who is considered the fastest triggerman in the NHL, waits for a face-off.

The Philadelphia Flyers successive Stanley Cup wins in 1974 and 1975 were rooted in the sheer determination of captain Bobby Clarke. His sweat-soaked hair and face reflect the energy he exerts.

Viewing the game from the bench does different things to different players. Veteran defenseman Terry Harper (left) appears calm compared to his more intense younger teammate Larry Brown.

178

A change of scenery often revives a wilting star. Bob Nevin, once the captain of the New York Rangers, was believed washed up when he was on Broadway. The Los Angeles Kings reclaimed Nevin from the brink of the minors and in 1974-75 he was the Kings' most effective forward.

Expansion–
The Game Grows

Just as they laughed at Christopher Columbus when he said the world was round, they laughed at Clarence Campbell when he said the NHL world *would* be round in 1967.

Prior to that time the National Hockey League was geographically and quantitatively flat. There were six teams—New York Rangers, Chicago Black Hawks, Boston Bruins, Toronto Maple Leafs, Montreal Canadiens and Detroit Red Wings. The teams operated in a relatively well contained area of southeastern Canada and northeastern and central United States. This produced an aura of parochialism about the NHL that non-hockey people labeled bush league.

Major league baseball, football and basketball had expanded nationwide in the United States; sooner or later hockey would have to follow suit. For years the NHL old guard had balked at expansion. It doubted that a game indigenous to cold climates could survive, let alone thrive, in places such as Atlanta, Georgia, Los Angeles, California or St. Louis, Missouri.

But a new breed of NHL owners took power in the sixties led by attorney William Jennings, president of the New York Rangers. They had confidence in hockey's pulling power and planted the seeds for a grand expansion tree that would blossom beginning in October 1967.

A few cautious owners feared that the addition of more than one or two teams would drain the available talent wells. They pleaded—in vain, as it turned out—against the grand plan. But the Jen-nings' *clique* prevailed and when the ice had cleared at the end of the 1965–66 season the NHL moguls convened and welcomed six—count 'em, six—brand-new big league hockey franchises.

On the West Coast in California there were Oakland (Seals) and Los Angeles (Kings). In the Midwest, St. Louis (Blues) and Minnesota (North Stars) and the East brought forth Pittsburgh (Penguins) and Philadelphia (Flyers). Each franchise cost $2,000,000 and in return the clubs received a spate of low-grade players with a sprinkling of near stars.

Philadelphia's Flyers seemed, at first, to pluck the best players in the hockey mart. Goalie Bernie Parent eventually would become a star. Defenseman Ed Van Impe was an unobtrusive but terribly effective backliner and forward Gary Dornhoefer had been searching for a proper stage for his talents. He found it at the Philadelphia Spectrum.

All of the expansion teams were lumped in the NHL's newly created West Division, in which the Flyers excelled. The pivotal victory that established Philadelphia as a threat was one against the vaunted Montreal Canadiens in Montreal. It was more than just a win because the decision clearly indicated that a brand-new team could prevail against the old guard.

"The expansion team *can* win," the Flyers' defenseman Larry Zeidel pointed out, "if it's hungrier than the established team. When we're hungry we get on top of the opposition and we keep the pressure on."

179

Philadelphia's triumph at the Forum was hailed at the time as an NHL milestone.

The St. Louis Blues, although they didn't accelerate as fast as the Flyers, also were able to turn in first-rate performances. St. Louis coach Scotty Bowman signed a few aging NHL aces such as former Canadiens' defenseman Doug Harvey and left wing Dickie Moore, and by play-off time they were hot enough to oust Philadelphia in the first round.

Bowman's Blues went to the Stanley Cup finals where they were wiped out in four straight games by the mighty Canadiens. But the Blues had muscle and they quickly deposed Philadelphia in 1968–69 as the power of the West Division.

St. Louis had Glenn Hall as goaltender and Hall still was the best. Harvey ranked among the best defensemen, but Bowman lacked offensive punch until he obtained Red Berenson from the New York Rangers in a one-sided trade. The University of Michigan graduate quickly established his superstar credentials by scoring six goals in one game against the Philadelphia Flyers and became the spirit of St. Louis hockey.

In 1969 the Blues collided with the Canadiens in the Stanley Cup finals and, once again, were shellacked in four straight games. The Boston Bruins, one of hockey's strongest clubs, skated against the Blues in the 1970 Cup finals and dispatched Bowman's skaters as easily as the Canadiens had in previous play-offs.

Still, the Blues were the envy of expansion. The Flyers, who relied too heavily on light horse, light checking skaters, sagged after the opening expansion season and didn't pose a serious threat to St. Louis for several years. The Minnesota North Stars occasionally challenged the Blues, but not for long.

The Los Angeles Kings started off like Gang Busters—second to Philadelphia—in 1967–68 and then petered out like a punctured balloon.

So did the Oakland Seals. The Bay Area representative was undercapitalized at the start and suffered through a long series of financial crises that seriously affected its winning capabilities. To a lesser degree, the same problem braked the Pittsburgh Penguins' progress. In the meantime, the NHL decided to expand again and in 1970 Buffalo and Vancouver were welcomed into the league.

George "Punch" Imlach, who had molded a Stanley Cup winning dynasty in Toronto, was imported by the Buffalo Sabres as their chief architect. This time Imlach, who became coach and manager of the new club, had to start from scratch and work with a collection of mediocrities supported by junior graduate Gil Perreault.

"You're here," Imlach told his men at training camp, "because nobody else wanted you. As far as I'm concerned, you don't have the ability to play for any other NHL team, or you wouldn't be here. But we'll even things up—with dedication, more hustle and being in better shape." Then, a pause and a determined stare. "We'll be competitive from our first game!"

Across the continent, manager Bud Poile was making a similar prediction about his just built Vancouver Canucks. Whereas Imlach had the complete backing of the brothers Northrup and Seymour Knox, the Sabres' owners, Poile was hassled by a Byzantine front office and inept coaching. Neither team showed much in its rookie season but, then again, little was expected of them.

So far, expansion was considerably more of a financial than an artistic success. St. Louis, Buffalo, Philadelphia, Vancouver and Minnesota regu-

The value of the NHL draft has been under-
scored by the fact that several of the players
claimed by the "have not" teams blossomed
in their new surroundings. One of them,
defenseman Bob Murdoch, languished in the
Montreal Canadiens' organization until he was
claimed by Los Angeles. He has since become
one of the most effective defensemen on the
Kings.

Once considered an awkward behemoth on
skates, Atlanta Flames' defenseman Pat Quinn
has over the years refined his skills and now is
one of the NHL's most respected backliners.

larly played to capacity crowds, but not one of the newer clubs seriously believed it could challenge for the Stanley Cup until it developed several young superstars. As luck would have it, the Flyers—original winners of the Clarence Campbell Bowl for supremacy in the West Division—came up with the ripest young talent the fastest.

The balance wheel of the Flyers turned out to be a gap-toothed diabetic named Bobby Clarke from the unlikely town of Flin Flon, Manitoba, just inside the Arctic Circle. Bypassed by other teams because of his condition, Clarke became an instant hero in Philadelphia and displayed qualities usually found in 10-year veterans.

Clarke, either in spite of or because of his diabetes, appeared capable of skating miles without becoming winded and stickhandling as if the puck was tied to his stick by invisible rope.

Led by Clarke's shooting stick and Parent's goalie stick, the Flyers matured into a team competitive with the best of the expansion clubs during the 1973–74 season. Coach Fred Shero proved to be a

nonpareil innovator whose creativity was as much responsible for the Flyers' climb as the acquisition of Clarke, Parent or another budding superstar, Rick MacLeish.

While other teams were run just by a coach and a manager, sometimes one and the same, Shero opted for special assistants. Shero felt that since they have assistants in other sports, why not in hockey. Former NHL goalie Marcel Pelletier advised Parent and longtime minor league forward Mike Nykoluk worked with forwards.

When defenseman Barry Ashbee sustained a serious eye injury in the 1974 play-offs in a game against the Rangers which ended his playing career, Shero hired him as a full-time defensive coach. All three assistants, however, were ordered to communicate information about every facet of play, not only their own specialty. "A coach," says Shero, "must know every system. They know exactly what I want. They have the right at any time to talk to a player about what he's doing wrong. They don't have to come to me. They can fine

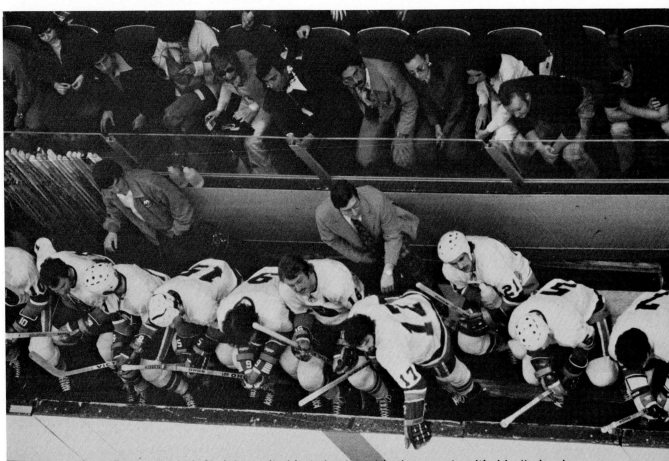

182

Bespectacled Al Arbour (behind the bench), the coach with his "miracle team," the New York Islanders, one of four expansion teams that turned in superior performances against original NHL clubs in the 1974-75 season. He has just signaled center Jude Drouin to the take the ice.

players, criticize them. I don't want a yes-man. As far as we can see, we almost have everything covered the best we know how to."

The Shero System paid its first major dividends in the 1973–74 season. Philadelphia defeated the established New York Rangers and then the Boston Bruins—the latter of which was fortified with superstars Bobby Orr and Phil Esposito—to win the Stanley Cup, the first expansion club to gain such glory.

It was, in fact, hard to believe. And some observers believed it was a fluke. "People are not convinced that we're for real," said Flyers' utility ace Terry Crisp. "They think we're a one-shot team." Then, as if to refute the critics, the Flyers marched headlong to first place in the Lester Patrick Division of the NHL in 1975, outpointing the Rangers, Bruins, Canadiens, in fact *every* established team in the league.

But the Flyers weren't alone. Their expansion compatriots, the Sabres, the Kings and the Canucks, also were climbing fast to the NHL's cloud nine. By far, the most rapid development was in Buffalo where the Sabres reached the play-offs in 1973, only their third year in the NHL.

The Sabres were eliminated by the Montreal Canadiens but not without giving the Flying Frenchmen a genuine scare. Imlach had constructed a formidable forward line comprised of Perreault, Rene Robert and Rick Martin. They were called "The French Connection" and scored 11 of Buffalo's 16 goals in the series.

Imlach continued building around the Connection, and by 1975 he had constructed one of the most exciting sextets ever to come down the pike. He needed a rock-ribbed defense and finally built it with the acquisition of such hulking skaters as Josh Guevremont, Jerry Korab and Jim Schoenfeld.

He also needed a solid second and third line to take the heat off the Connection. He got that by aligning center Fred Stanfield with Jim Lorentz and lacrosse star Rick Dudley, as well as center Don Luce with Craig Ramsey and Danny Gare. Veteran goalie Roger Crozier, an original member of the Sabres, continued with them through the 1975 play-offs but he was relieved by young Gary Bromley and another veteran, Gerry Desjardins.

"This club," said Imlach on the eve of the 1975 Cup round, "will win the Stanley Cup . . . eventual-

One of the geniuses among hockey front office men, George "Punch" Imlach built a dynasty in Toronto and more recently moved to Buffalo where he developed the Sabres from a helpless expansion team into 1975 Stanley Cup finalists.

ly. We now have the talent; all we're lacking is the experience."

Imlach's rookie coach Floyd Smith dazzled the more experienced ice generals across the rink with his strategy and leadership. The Sabres wiped out coach Bill Reay's Chicago Black Hawks in the opening round of the 1975 play-offs and then shellacked the Canadiens, four games to two in the semifinals.

The Sabres had come of age. But so had the Kings. Ridiculed for his club's ineptitude, Los Angeles owner Jack Kent Cooke cleaned house in 1974 and hired Jake Milford as manager and Bob Pulford as coach. The overbearing Cooke already had gone through six coaches in eight years and many critics doubted that Pulford, a learned man who had starred for the Toronto Maple Leafs, would have a positive effect on the Los Angeles skaters.

Milford knew that changes had to be made and he made them. First, he acquired four young members of the New York Rangers, Mike Murphy, Tommy Williams, Gene Carr and Sheldon Kannegiesser   183

184

Reggie Leach, Bobby Clarke's old pal from Flin Flon, Manitoba, added pep to the Flyers' attack in their march to the 1975 Stanley Cup triumph against the Buffalo Sabres.

Phil Myre, once a second string goaltender
with the Montreal Canadiens, matured into a
first rate ace playing for the Atlanta Flames.
Myre earned wide respect for his kick saves.

whom he aligned with veteran defenseman Terry Harper and goalie Rogatien Vachon.

"When I first came to L.A. we didn't believe in ourselves," says Vachon. "If we played Boston, we expected to lose. We only wanted to make a good showing. Now, it's a whole new game. I used to think we were really bad, but the coach never gave up on us. If it wasn't for him, it really would have been tough."

The Kings officially stopped playing like knaves in the 1974–75 season. They skated neck and neck with the Canadiens for first place in the James Norris Division, finishing a strong second. Vachon was so good that many railbirds began comparing him favorably to the magnificent Bernie Parent.

West Coast hockey got another boost that year when the Vancouver Canucks, once the laughing stock of Canada, suddenly developed under manager-coach Phil Maloney. Like the Kings, Vancouver's entry revolved around its goalkeeper; in this case behemoth Gary "Suitcase" Smith. They had staying power, surviving serious injuries to beat out the established Chicago Black Hawks for first place in the Conn Smythe Division.

Meanwhile, the NHL's expansion machinery had continued to turn and in 1972 two more franchises were admitted, the Atlanta Flames and New York Islanders. Both entries were unknown qualities before the first puck was dropped in their maiden seasons. Atlanta represented the first pro hockey venture into the deep South on an ambitious big league level. There were those who doubted that Southerners would welcome the Canadian sport. The Islanders, playing in the new Nassau Veterans Memorial Coliseum on Long Island, just east of New York City faced a different challenge. They were invading territory up until then the domain of the established New York Rangers. Could the New York City area support two NHL franchises?

Answers to both questions were supplied before the 1972–73 season was half over. Coached by the ebullient French Canadian Bernie "Boom Boom" Geoffrion, the Flames captured the hearts of Georgians and proved considerably more competitive than the equally young Islanders. But the baby New York entry, though a consistent loser, played to ever growing crowds and by the end of the season had won the hearts and enthusiasm of

Long Islanders the way the New York Mets had a decade earlier.

Amazingly, the Flames gained a play-off berth in their second season while the Islanders made headway after signing gifted young defenseman Denis Potvin. Win or lose, both new entries had proven they were here to stay. Now the question was—how long would it take them to become serious challengers for the Stanley Cup.

Although the Flames appeared to have had the inside track because of their early success it was the Islanders who stunned the NHL's Lester Patrick Division a year later. In a breathtaking late season race with the Flames, the Islanders not only edged Atlanta but came within a point of taking second place away from the venerable Rangers.

The Islanders' great leap forward was the work of general manager Bill Torrey and coach Al Arbour. Torrey fumbled the puck in his first season—hence the Islanders' nickname, Torrey's Turkeys—and appeared destined for oblivion. "Every time someone wrote about us," Torrey remembers with a smile, "they always preceded our name with hapless. After a while I thought our club was the Hapless Islanders instead of New York Islanders."

But the acquisition of Potvin, the maturing of speedy forward Billy Harris and the mellowing influence of Arbour put the Islanders on the right track in their second year and by 1974–75 they were roaring full speed ahead. They met the vaunted Rangers in the opening play-off round and stunned the established team from Broadway with a two-games-to-one play-off victory, scoring the winning goal in sudden-death overtime. Then, they took on the Pittsburgh Penguins. In seven previous seasons the Penguins never had come close to winning as many games as they lost. In the 1974–75 season they became an offensive juggernaut that finished at 37–28–15, the sixth-best regular season record in the 18-team NHL.

In the first round of the 1975 play-offs the Penguins knocked off the St. Louis Blues in two straight games. Then, thanks to the superb goaltending of Gary Inness, they streaked to three straight wins over the Islanders. Super confident, the Penguins began looking ahead to the next series, against the Stanley Cup champion Flyers.

Then something strange happened.

The Islanders won the fourth game of the series, played at Nassau Coliseum. When the fifth game in Pittsburgh was over the Islanders had won again. Unstoppable, Torrey's former Turkeys swept the sixth game and, astonishingly, the seventh and final game. They had won four straight play-off games after losing the first three. Only one other team—the 1942 Toronto Maple Leafs—had ever accomplished such a Herculean feat.

There was only one stumbling block to the Cup; the Islanders were to meet the Flyers in the semi-final round and the champs set Arbour's young sextet reeling. One, two, three, the Flyers defeated the Islanders. Only a dyed-in-the-wool optimist such as Torrey could see some humor in the debacle. "Now," he said, his fist clenched, "we've got 'em where we want 'em."

In the fourth game of the series played in the Nassau Coliseum the Islanders finally won a game. Upon returning to the friendly confines of the Spectrum, the Flyers expected to annex the series in the fifth game. But the Islanders overwhelmed Philadelphia, 5–1, as Goalie Resch shut out the stunned Flyers for 55 minutes.

The sixth game, back in Long Island. Although Philadelphia took an early 1–0 lead, the Islanders characteristically pulled themselves together and counterattacked. They tied the score in the second period and won the game 2–1 with a goal in the third.

By now the entire sporting world had taken the three-year-old Islanders to their hearts as they embarked for Philadelphia and the seventh and final game of the series. No team in any professional sport ever had won two consecutive championship series back to back after being down three games to none in both.

And it wasn't to happen this time as the Flyers took the series by winning 4–3.

The man behind a miracle: When the New York Islanders captivated hockey fans in 1975 with their stirring come-from-behind play-off victory over Pittsburgh, considerable credit was accorded Islanders' manager Bill Torrey. In three seasons, Torrey organized an inept club into a serious aspirant for the Stanley Cup.

The Islanders' unexpected flowering overshadowed another major accomplishment for the expansionists. Buffalo defeated Montreal four games to two which meant that each of the teams in the 1975 Stanley Cup finals was an expansion club, a first for the NHL.

This gave heart to those who ridiculed the Washington (D.C.) Capitals and Kansas City Scouts, the expansion babies of 1974–75. The Capitals, in particular, suffered terribly in the standings but, like their predecessors, they looked ahead with optimism.

And well they might. After all, look at what Torrey's Turkeys had accomplished in only three years of existence. The NHL had proven that expansion could work. Proved it with arithmetic. During the 1974–75 season, the league set an attendance record, attracting one million more fans than ever before. Total attendance was 9,521,536, surpassing the previous mark of 8,640,978. Even the big losers were winners: Kansas City and Washington, the two new clubs and the ones most defeated, had a combined total attendance of 673,586.

188

Youngsters and journeymen play side by side as hockey clubs mix the spirit and speed of promising novices with the wisdom and background of veterans. Center Bobby Lalonde of Vancouver stickhandles forward while veteran Leon Rochefort, 12 years his senior, brings up the rear.

The new breed. Tom Lysiak, the husky Atlanta Flames forward, was a serious contender for the NHL rookie-of-the-year award in 1974, losing out to Denis Potvin of the Islanders. However, Lysiak made it clear that he will be a formidable attacking force in seasons to come.

When two muscle men meet—Bobby Orr (No. 4) and Dale Rolfe—the result is a standoff.

While Buffalo's Bill Hajt and the Flyers' Bill Barber struggle for the puck in the corner of the rink, Don Saleski opportunistically follows through and frees the disk. Lee Fogolin (right) moves in on Saleski.

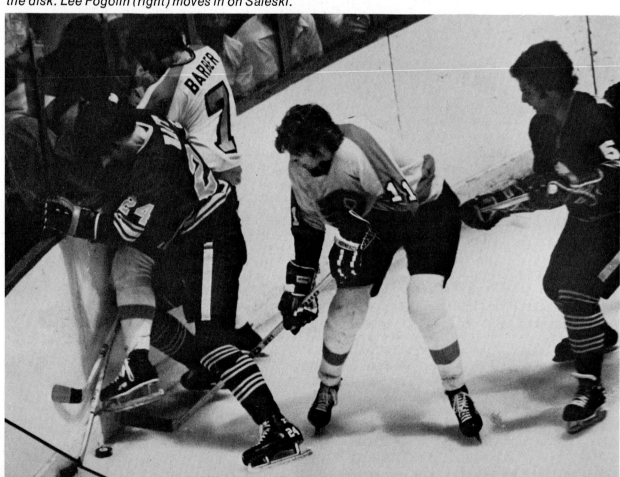

Gil Perreault, like most hockey league players who are missing teeth (and that includes almost all of the professionals), leaves his false teeth in the dressing room when he takes to the ice.

When a goalie goes down to block a shot the shooter should attempt to find air above the fallen netminder. The Cleveland Crusaders' Skip Krake sees the two feet of space along the top and blasts the rubber over the Winnipeg Jets' goaltender.

Peter Mahovlich's older brother Frank Mahovlich skated alongside his frere with the Canadiens. Frank, alias The Big M, jumped to the Toronto Toros of the WHA before the 1974-75 season.

WHA
A New Challenge

The formation and growth of the World Hockey Association in the 1970s had more impact on the structure of professional ice hockey than any other single factor in the previous three decades. With competition for players both from newly formed NHL clubs and WHA teams, salaries skyrocketed. The game spread into new areas, and many sports enthusiasts became acquainted with hockey for the first time. Another result was the first all-out interleague hockey war in decades.

Credit for forming and developing the WHA has to go to Dennis Murphy and Gary Davidson, both of whom were also instrumental in the creation of the American Basketball Association. The fact that the NHL ruled the roost as the only major professional hockey league seemed to both annoy and inspire Murphy and Davidson. Seeing gold at the end of the hockey rainbow, they decided they could provide the long established NHL with some fancy competition. On June 10, 1971, the World Hockey Association was incorporated. In many ways, hockey hasn't been the same since then.

Once the NHL moguls stopped laughing at the new kid on the block, they decided to punish him.

First, they drew up a battle plan. They would ignore the WHA, just pretend it didn't even exist.

Before long, however, the WHA had placed teams in Houston, Cleveland, St. Paul, New York, Los Angeles, Ottawa, Quebec City, Boston, Philadelphia, Chicago, Winnipeg and Edmonton.

The new league then pursued some of the NHL's finest talent, stars such as Bobby Hull, Bernie Parent and Derek Sanderson. They didn't get every man they went after, but the WHA made quite a dent in the rosters of many an NHL club.

In June 1972 Bobby Hull signed with the Winnipeg Jets for $2,750,000 over a ten-year period as a player-coach. J. C. Tremblay left the Canadiens for the Quebec Nordiques and Gerry Cheevers jumped to Cleveland.

That perennial All-Stars and top drawing cards were jumping to the WHA angered NHL bigwigs, but they still refused to regard the newcomers as a serious threat to their monopoly. What irritated Clarence Campbell and associates were the high salaries and bonuses being offered by the WHA to every NHLer worth his weight in dollar bills, as well as some who weren't.

The WHA was sprinkled with a few NHL stars that first season, but mostly was loaded with journeymen and minor leaguers. These mediocre players were collecting paychecks far in excess of their worth.

What the WHA lacked in talent it tried to make up in rule changes. Among them—allowing player-coaches, playing a 10-minute sudden death overtime period in tie games, no "third man in" rule in a fight and no icing the puck on a penalty unless the player so doing carries the puck over the blue line.

The WHA also persuaded both CBS and the Canadian Broadcasting Company to carry some games, a major step for a brand new league. Unfortunately, the WHA lost its television contract after that first year.

The Boston based New England Whalers won the AVCO World Trophy in 1973 to become the WHA champions by defeating the Hull-led Jets in five games. As expected, the Golden Jet was the league's most valuable player although he failed to win the scoring title, which went to Andrew Lacroix of the Philadelphia Blazers.

While the first WHA season could be termed a success for the Whalers and a few others (notably the Minnesota Fighting Saints and the Cleveland Crusaders) quite a number of outfits were on very shaky footing. The Philadelphia Blazers, who had paid a vast sum to Derek Sanderson, lost him early in the campaign. Bernie Parent also left the Blazers during the play-offs. Both Sanderson and Parent returned to the NHL. The Ottawa Nationals moved to Toronto and the Blazers to Vancouver, respectively. In those cities, the new teams attempted to go head-on in competition for fan support, in the same arenas, with teams from the older circuit.

Into its second season, the WHA continued its battle with the NHL for players, and salaries continued to skyrocket. In perhaps its best move the league signed the legendary Gordie Howe who played for the Houston Aeros from 1973 to 1975. The WHA raided the junior Canadian leagues by signing underage youngsters, contrary to previous agreements between the professional hockey world (the NHL) and the amateurs. Among the many teenagers inked to WHA pacts were Gordie's sons Mark and Marty and this was as much responsible for their father's return to the ice as the large monetary inducement.

Gordie led the Aeros to two consecutive titles.

Ben Hatskin, the man who convinced Hull to jump to the Jets, is now the Chairman of the Board of Governors and leader of the WHA. Davidson disappeared in October 1973 to head up the World Football League, and Murphy resigned following the WHA's third season.

Prior to the league's third campaign in 1974, the WHA All-Stars took on the Soviet team that had surprised the NHL's Team Canada contingent in 1972. When Team Canada 74 managed a win and a tie in the series' first two encounters, the WHA seemed headed for a victory that would make the sports world heed the league as a genuine professional competitor to the NHL.

Whenever the Soviets take the ice they are a force to be reckoned with, and the WHA stars couldn't handle the sudden ferocity the Russians displayed in the third game in Winnipeg, an 8–5 Soviet triumph that set the stage for their taking four of the final six contests, with two ties, for a 4–1–3 advantage.

Considering the competition, the WHA is doing as well as any new league can expect.

Several unsung NHL heroes jumped to the WHA and enjoyed instant fame. One of them was Gary Jarrett who became a star in Cleveland with the Crusaders.

Bobby Hull, hockey's Golden Jet, got himself a new league in 1972—the WHA—and a new team, the Winnipeg Jets, as well as a new hairpiece. The former Chicago Black Hawks' star, more than any other single player, was responsible for the success of the new league. Hull's booming slap shot continues to draw crowds; his speed has hardly diminished. Bobby's rugged physique has also kept him among the sexiest players and his unending devotion to kids makes him a favorite with autograph seeking youngsters wherever he skates.

Hockey is a small man's game as well as a big man's sport and nobody proves it better than little Dave Keon who for years has been captain and the stalwart center of the Toronto Maple Leafs. Keon is regarded as one of the fastest skaters in the NHL.

Syl Apps of the Pittsburgh Penguins veers towards an opening in the New York Rangers' defense guarded by Gilles Marotte.

The attacker vs. the defense. When enemy forwards confront the backliners, the defensemen try to work in tandem to prevent the attackers from exploiting any opening. Here Buffalo Sabre defenders execute a pincer movement against an attempted blitzkrieg by Montreal's Peter Mahovlich.

The ups and downs of hockey. Brad Selwood, a New England Whalers' defenseman, finds himself in a hockey version of being behind the eight ball. Selwood is temporarily trapped under the net which became dislodged from the upright pipes that hold it in place.

Hockey— Zany and Human

Is hockey zanier than other sports? Is there something intrinsic in the ice game that produces a fan such as Pete Cusimano of Detroit who regularly would bring a *live* octopus to the Red Wings' games at Olympia Stadium and then toss it onto the rink for good luck?

Of course hockey is different from and zanier than other sports and what's more it is as zany in the seventies as it was in the sixties or the fifties, in fact, as far back as the 19th century. During hockey's earliest days in the late 1800s it was not uncommon for a game to be postponed because of melted ice. Rinks did not have artificial icemaking equipment at the turn of the century. So, if spring came early, there went the hockey season.

Yet, in 1975 when scientists had already placed men on the moon, two Stanley Cup final games between Philadelphia and Buffalo nearly were postponed on account of fog. The bizarre apparition of a dense London-type fog overhanging Memorial Auditorium in Buffalo developed on the night of May 20, 1975 when the temperature at ice level was 90 degrees Fahrenheit.

There were no octopi on the ice but a bat flew out of the catacombs of the arena, swooped over the players and finally was struck down by Rick MacLeish of the Flyers, who swung through the fog.

The fog developed because of the mixture of high temperatures and humidity encouraged by a lack of proper ventilation and no air conditioning. The fog reached such pea soup intensity by midpoint in the contest that 12 times in the last 33 minutes referee Lloyd Gilmour had to halt the action. Even zanier was the sight of players skating around the rink during the respites to stir up the air and make the steam rise from the ice.

"A guy could get killed in those conditions," said Flyers' coach Fred Shero. And, in fact, his goalie Bernie Parent almost *did* get killed by 125 mile per hour shots whizzing past his head (as well as past Buffalo goalie Roger Crozier's head) through the fog.

Buffalo won the game, 5-4, on the shot by Rene Robert which goalie Parent never saw because of the fog. When the teams played in Buffalo two nights later the fog returned, and fortunately so did the players' sense of humor. "We could," said Philadelphia forward Terry Crisp, "wear miner's helmets with flashlights, paint the puck orange and put a lighthouse above the net."

Buffalo defenseman Larry Carriere thought he had a better idea. "We could tie electric fans to our backs," said Carriere, "and skate around."

For some players the fog was the most trying hockey experience of their careers. "It was brutal out there," said Buffalo defenseman Jerry Korab. "With the heat so bad, and the fog, it was hard to breathe. I lost ten pounds, at least."

It was, of course, worse for the goalies who wore 40 pounds of equipment as well as stifling masks, and were dripping with sweat. "When the winning goal was scored," said goalie Parent, "I saw three guys coming at me through the fog. I didn't even know which one had the puck. I lost it in the fog and never saw the shot that went in."

Goalies don't require fog to drive them to distraction; their occupation is enough. One of the best of today's big league netminders has been seeing a psychiatrist and one of the best of the last decade's netminders had also been known to seek professional counseling.

Veteran goalie Gump Worsley of the Montreal Canadiens, later with the Minnesota North Stars and now retired, thought nothing of standing unflinchingly in front of blazing shots, but he had an obsessive fear of flying. Somehow Worsley managed to cope with the strain until 1967, when the NHL expanded to 12 teams and he was compelled to fly from coast to coast with the Canadiens. During the 1968–69 season Worsley finally cracked. He told manager Sammy Pollock that he had had it! No more flying, no more playing. Pollock persuaded Gump to see a psychiatrist to cope with his fear of flying.

"We talked a lot," said Worsley. "He tried to work me through it. He helped a lot. Pretty soon I felt not bad."

Worsley returned to the goal and played a key role in the Canadiens' winning of the Stanley Cup that spring.

Surely as unnerving, if not as zany, as the goalie's life is the yo-yo-like career of a third-string player who finds himself traded from team to team almost every season. "It's brutal, really brutal," says defenseman Larry Hillman, who has the distinction of being the most traded player in big league hockey. "Every time I got traded it shocked the hell out of me. I just couldn't believe it was happening."

Hillman was traded so many times that the law of averages finally caught up with him and he got a break on the positive side. That happened in 1968 when he was playing for the Minnesota North Stars and was quite content with life, or as content as a third-stringer could be.

But one day a rumor circulated around the North Stars' dressing room that a player would be traded the next day. "Either I'm gonna get mad," thought Hillman, "or I've got to learn to live with it."

Like most players, Hillman feared that he would be sent to Oakland, then owned by erratic sports-

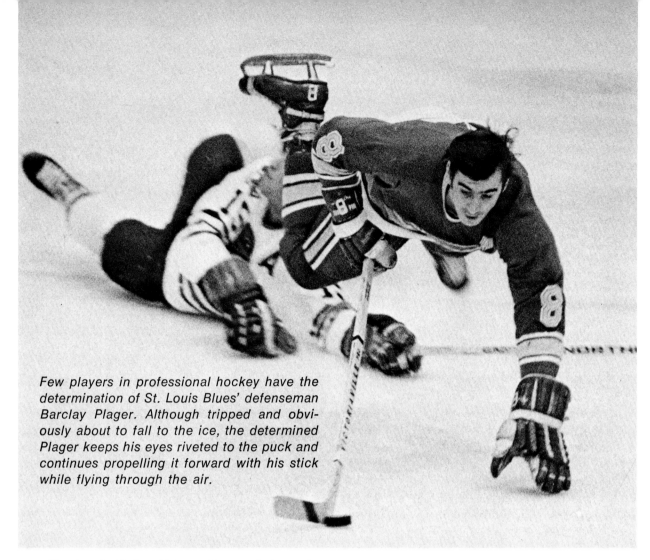

Few players in professional hockey have the determination of St. Louis Blues' defenseman Barclay Plager. Although tripped and obviously about to fall to the ice, the determined Plager keeps his eyes riveted to the puck and continues propelling it forward with his stick while flying through the air.

man Charles O. Finley. "I hope it's not Oakland," one teammate said. "Finley will drive you crazy."

The next day Hillman walked into the manager's office. He *had* been the traded player. But ten minutes later he walked out of the office, beaming like a Cheshire cat. "Everybody's jaw dropped," Hillman recalls. "Here they were all ready to offer me a prayer because I was heading for Oakland, the last stop on the way to hell. Instead, I'm heading to Montreal for a Stanley Cup."

Luck was on Hillman's side. The Canadiens, with Larry on defense, won the Stanley Cup. With the bonus money he bought nine acres of land in St. Catherines, Ontario. But he didn't last long in Montreal. He soon moved on to Philadelphia, then Buffalo and eventually Cleveland of the World Hockey Association. "Things could've been worse," says the most traded big leaguer. Then, recalling that during one season *he had been owned by five different NHL teams,* Hillman philosophized: "It may be that my greatest accomplishment has been my survival."

The same could be said for Larry's brother, Wayne, who had done a similar tour of duty. In fact the Hillmans played on so many different teams that every once in a while their paths would cross. They played together in Minnesota, Philadelphia and Cleveland, which is more than some other brother acts can say.

The Bentley Brothers, for example—Max and Doug—skated together in Chicago and later in New York while the Plagers—Bob, Barclay and, for a time, Bill—teamed up on the St. Louis Blues' defense. Brother acts have been sprinkled through hockey from the earliest days. In contemporary hockey the Hextalls—Dennis and Bryan—and the Espositos—Phil and Tony—are among the more accomplished players.

But through the years only one family has continually dominated the game—the Patrick clan. It began with Joseph Patrick who built the first artificial ice rinks in Canada in Vancouver and Victoria. The sons of Joseph Patrick, Lester and Frank, organized the Pacific Coast League in 1912.

Lester eventually moved East and organized the first New York Rangers' dynasty and continued to run the Broadway Blueshirts from 1926 to 1946. Brother Frank was equally important, having introduced the blue lines and forward pass to hockey in 1915. Previously, only lateral or drop passes had been allowed and games were repeatedly interrupted by offside calls. Frank Patrick divided the ice into thirds and produced rules which eventually were adopted by the NHL.

The Patrick clan continued to make hockey news when Lester's sons, Lynn and Muzz, played for their dad on the Rangers. At first New York fans charged Lester with nepotism when Lynn put on a Rangers' uniform in 1934. "My dad merely said that if I was good enough, I'd stay," Lynn recalls, "and if I wasn't, then he certainly wasn't going to keep me around."

Lynn spent ten years in a Rangers' uniform. Muzz was signed three years after his older brother and also enjoyed a lengthy stay in New York.

It wasn't until expansion that the fourth generation of Patricks emerged in the hockey news. Craig Patrick, Lynn's son, played for the U.S. Olympic Team, the University of Denver and finally the NHL's California Seals and, more recently, the St. Louis Blues of which his father is a vice-president.

Another of Lynn's sons, Glenn, played defense for Salt Lake City of the Central League in the 1974–75 season while a third son, Dean, starred in St. Louis high school and junior hockey. "There always have been Patricks in important positions in hockey," says Craig. "I certainly didn't feel that being part of the family was an overwhelming load to carry. It was more a feeling of great pride that the family had accomplished so much."

There's nothing wrong with familial pride in hockey but, until 1975, there *was* something bizarre about sexual pride—male vs. female—in on-the-ice accomplishments. By that year organized women's hockey had not only become a fact of life on the ice but women sportswriters also had crashed the dressing room barrier, interviewing both NHL and WHA players in the semi-nude—and sometimes nude—following games, along with their male counterparts.

Even more interesting was the organized female hockey league which reached its peak in quality play in Michigan and Ontario, where females are

With the passing years more and more women are taking up hockey as a participant sport. In some areas of the United States and Canada women play in highly organized leagues. One outstanding team is the Point Edward Supremes located near the city of Sarnia, Ontario. Like their male counterparts the female skaters wear helmets, gauntlets and regulation hockey skates.

playing a bruising and fast brand of hockey that would make even Dave Schultz blush. The six team Michigan-Ontario Ladies' Hockey League has everything the NHL has, including fights, artistry and an international (Canada vs. United States) rivalry.

"They *are* ladies," says Lenora Dunham, president of the Michigan-Ontario Ladies' Hockey League. "But they're also hockey players and they lose their tempers just as quickly as men. There are no polite tea party manners when they have trouble on the ice—just the old five knuckles in the chops."

The female counterpart of NHL penalty-leader

Schultz has been Debbie Hands who plays for the Point Edward Supremes. Point Edward is officially an Ontario village of 3,000, but according to league president Dunham "just a spit across the street and you're in Sarnia." Sarnia is an industrial city of 60,000 which looks upon the Supremes with paternal pride. The Supremes, in turn, play the game just as intensely as the male teams in town. "I go out there to win not lose," says Debbie Hands. "Sometimes that means taking a player out. I just don't back down easy, that's all."

According to the Canadian ladies, the American teams are more demure in their attitude about hockey. "Every time you check the Americans," says Supremes' goalie Debbie Gibson, "they lay down and cry."

Organized hockey among women is becoming so popular across the continent that girls are attending summer hockey schools and in some cases playing on men's teams. Even sports equipment manufacturers are marketing special equipment for the ladies. "It can hurt," says one of the Supremes, "if you get a puck in the crotch. The trouble is, a girl can't grab herself and howl the way a boy can. It wouldn't look good."

To solve that problem CCM, the sports equipment manufacturer, is marketing a *Jill Strap,* plus a chest protector with cups to accommodate breasts.

Who knows, maybe the next item will be an anti-fog machine and an octopus catcher, and perhaps hockey will be a little less zany than before.

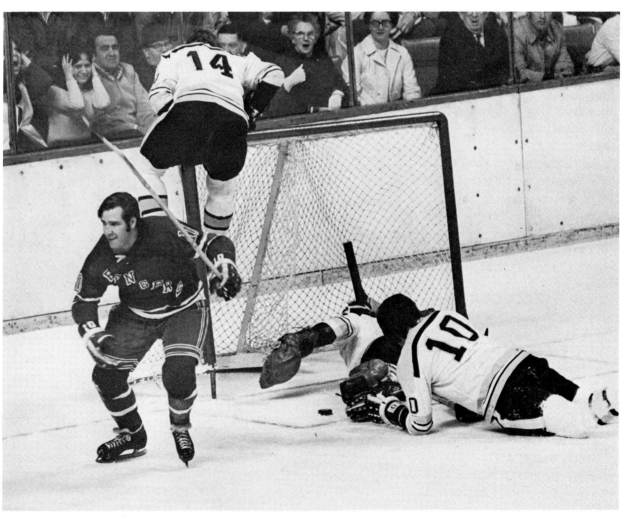

Ups and downs: The Boston Bruins' goalie and defenseman are down. Another Bruin forward is up (climbing the net) but it is all in vain as the New York Rangers' Bill Fairbairn has just scored.

Ice hockey is becoming more popular as a competitive sport in colleges and universities. Some of the rules are different and the college game is not as rough as the professional game. Here, in an East Coast Athletic Conference tournament Cornell plays Boston College.

207

*Guess who scored? The Black Hawks, led by
Stan Mikita (center).*

Rangers on the bench (above) watch as goalie Eddie Giacomin (below) assumes a rather undignified position.

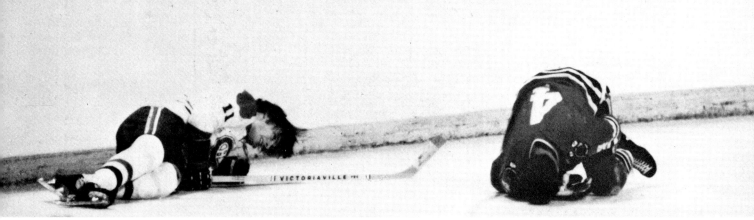

When the irresistible force meets the immovable object on ice, this is the result during a game between the Montreal Canadiens and the Chicago Black Hawks.

On the inside looking out Jean Potvin, the Islanders' defenseman, and Ross Lonsberry of the Flyers jam against the boards inside the rink and appear to be looking for a way out.

In trying to select a particular player upon whom to focus in a book that tells what hockey is all about, one comes to the inevitable conclusion that the most significant personality and also, the outstanding performer, in the period beginning with the end of World War II and continuing into the 1970s was undoubtedly Gordon (Gordie) Howe. Howe made hockey history with his scoring and a continuing high standard of excellence. After his official playing days were over, he moved into the presidency of the Houston Aeros. Below: The playing members of the Howe family when they skated together with the Aeros. Left to Right: Gordie, Marty, Mark.

The Remarkable Howes

It is unfortunate that in dealing with the accomplishments of Gordie Howe and his sons, Mark and Marty, once useful adjectives—superb, tremendous, amazing, great—are incapable of putting the Howes' feats in proper perspective.

Someone will have to invent a new set of clichés to correctly describe the Howes' contribution to the game of hockey, historically, artistically and, in a sense, financially.

The family pillar is Gordie himself, who broke in with the Detroit Red Wings during the 1946–47 season and remains the only athlete in American history to have spanned—and starred in—three distinct sporting eras. He retired from the Red Wings in 1971 and returned to the game with the Houston Aeros in 1973.

He insisted upon retiring at the start of the 1975–76 season after a token appearance with the Aeros for the opening of the new 16,000 seat Summit Arena in Houston.

Sometime around the year 2000, when hockey fans are having a "hot stove" discussion, Gordie Howe will, by then, be recognized as the greatest all-around player who ever lived. He has achieved that distinction already, having scored more goals and more assists than any man in the history of big league hockey. But time will embellish Howe's stature because it is becoming increasingly obvious that none of his contemporaries had the versatility or the artistry of Howe.

Other sports have known their Methuselahs. Baseball had Warren Spahn and football, Lou Groza, but neither was tested in so grueling an activity as playing right wing and going full tilt for more than 30 minutes a game as Howe does. "Howe may be the most marvelous of all," wrote Detroit Free Press sports editor Joe Falls. "For while the great Spahn went out there every third, fourth or fifth day and while the great Groza restricted himself to placekicking and maybe making two tackles a game, the amazing Howe has been out there, game after game, season after season, losing a step here and a stride there, but maintaining so many of his skills that some nights he is still unquestionably the best player on the ice."

What is Gordie's secret for staying so active both on the ice and in his many office activities?

"Let me tell you a story," Howe explained. "I was fishing in Saskatchewan one time and we had an Indian guide who was 68. We came to a cliff that was maybe 20 feet high. He walked up to it and jumped off and I said to myself that if a man that old could do it, then I should be able to. But he had the know-how, see. I didn't, and nearly killed myself. In hockey, if you can figure out where the puck is going to go, or how a play is going to develop, you can save a lot of energy by skating to where you're going to be needed. If I had any secret, that's it."

Gordie launched his professional career in 1945 with the Omaha Knights. In May 1975—an awesome 30 years later—Howe scored two goals and assisted on a third as he directed the Houston Aeros to their second consecutive World Hockey Association championship. What's more, he was skating like a colt although he was close to his forty-eighth birthday. And he was as tough as he

211

had been in his halcyon days with the Red Wings.

The Howe legend began in April 1950 when he was carried from the ice at Olympia Stadium in Detroit following a collision with Ted Kennedy of the Toronto Maple Leafs. Although it was feared that Howe (a) might not live or (b) if he did, would never play hockey again, Gordie returned to lead the NHL in scoring the following year. From that point on the sky was his limit and the ice his kingdom.

From the time of the retirement of Maurice "Rocket" Richard in 1960, Gordie reigned as monarch of the ice. When King Gordie temporarily stepped off the throne prior to the 1971–72 season, he created a void which remained unfilled.

Could anyone ever follow Al Jolson? Or the Marx Brothers? Or the Beatles? No way.

When Gordie Howe retired from the Detroit Red Wings in 1971 after 25 years, 1,687 games and 1,809 points, there was only one man alive who could follow that act. That was Gordie Howe. The WHA, the new major circuit, had been formed and Gordie Howe returned to the ice at age 45. His sons, Marty and Mark, signed to skate alongside Pop with the Houston Aeros. Then the three Howes led Houston to the AVCO World Cup and the WHA title in 1974.

The scenario was so exciting it was scary—even for Howe. Gordie was the WHA's most valuable player; Mark was the rookie-of-the-year and Marty was unofficially hailed as the best young defenseman in the WHA as well as one of the game's most rugged body checkers. Mostly, it was Gordie's return at an advanced age for an athlete that stunned the hockey world.

It's one thing to make a comeback, but how many make that comeback *and* become the league's third leading scorer? Only King Gordie. And he led his team to a first place finish and play-off championship!

It's one thing to have your kids sign fat contracts. Lots of kids do, but how many make it? Marty, the defenseman, and Mark, the left wing, could pass for the best two youngsters in big league hockey. Gordie, easily, was the best oldster on skates.

Olympia Stadium was a shinny (hockey) concentration camp for Gordie in his last years with the Red Wings. The Jim Bishop-Ned Harkness regime turned him off, made him feel uncomfortable and unwanted.

He had a bone and a half taken out of his left wrist and he couldn't move it. He had accomplished what he wanted in the NHL and had suc-

In his prime Gordie Howe (No. 9) was the most accomplished forward in the game. As a leader of the Detroit Red Wings Howe here outbattles the Boston Bruins.

Gordie racked up 1,809 points and scored 786 goals in 1,687 games over 25 years of play with the Detroit Red Wings. He also appeared in 154 Stanley Cup play-off games and accrued 158 points in Cup play in nineteen of his Detroit years. Here he is engaged in 1963 action against the Toronto Maple Leafs.

cess. The Red Wings moved him into the front office and he felt he was given a job with nothing to do.

Then the WHA was born and Houston's Aeros offered Gordie a million dollars to play alongside Mark and Marty. By 1973 the old war horse was at it again.

"Dad plays better than he did in Detroit his last two seasons there," said Mark, who skated on the same line with his father and center Jim Sherritt. "He was happier playing with Marty and me, and it's easier being in first place than near the bottom."

Make no mistake, Gordie was not the Howe who had won six NHL Hart Trophies. He was a stride slower, but a stride wiser. His shot had less whammo and injuries inspired him to put a bit of a curve in his formerly flat stick. But when he skated at a foe, he was the same Gordie Howe who once pulverized NHL heavyweight champion Lou (Rangers) Fontinato and anybody else who dared challenge him.

"Gordie," said defenseman Carl Brewer, who once teamed with Howe on the Red Wings, "is the dirtiest player who ever lived. A great player, but also the dirtiest. He'll gouge your eye out if you give him a chance, carve you up. He's big and tough and uses his size to intimidate guys."

Gordie had heard such charges about his lack of proper decorum for more than a decade. He shrugged them off. His traditional retort—"Hockey is a man's game"—was altered with time. "I play tough," said Gordie, "but I never deliberately hurt anybody."

Occasionally an enemy policeman tried to cuff King Gordie. It's like the guy who wants to be able to tell his grandchildren that he once gave it to the Godfather. Ted Scharf, the notorious brawler, took a run at Gordie one night. "I'm not worried about Gordie Howe," said Scharf. "I know I can't scare him. He's not going to run from me. But he'll only play for another year or so. Some of these other guys see me running at Howe and they'll show respect for me in the future."

Respect is something Mark and Marty Howe have sought, and earned. Lean and tough, Marty adds a little mustard to every body check he throws. Mark skates a diligent left wing, often more conscious about defensive play than goal scoring.

"We've always had to show we're good hockey players and not just the sons of Gordie Howe," says Mark. "I hope now that the people will come to see me play because of the kind of player I am."

Mark had been hailed at age 19 as one of the best left wingers in big league hockey while Marty was regarded as one of the sport's top young defensemen.

Mark, in 1973–74, finished 14th in the WHA scoring race, and second among the rookies, with 38 goals and 41 assists for 79 points. Defenseman Marty scored four goals, adding 20 assists for 24 points.

Gordie made his debut with the kids September 25, 1973, playing in the WHA spectacular at Madison Square Garden. Less than a minute after he stepped on the ice, he scored a goal.

He received the standing bravos only he deserved. But the decibel count didn't fool Gordie. His muscles were rusty and his timing off. It was this way during the early weeks of the season. Once, during a practice, he crashed headfirst into the boards and took on the ashen appearance of a corpse.

But he rebounded, and with each week gained more speed and more points. When the season ended the Aeros were champs of the WHA's Western Division. Howe had scored 31 goals and 69 assists for 100 points, third best in the WHA. He starred against the Russians in the September 1974 international exhibition and then finished eighth in scoring during the 1974–75 season at the age of 47.

He says of himself, "I changed as I got older. The speed, the stamina wasn't there in 1975 the way it used to be when I was younger. The shot wasn't as hard, the reactions weren't as good and the recuperative powers weren't there."

Yet, in the 1975 WHA play-off finals against the Quebec Nordiques, Gordie appeared to be the strongest man on the ice, the way he was in 1965 and 1955. "He has always been the same way," said Rejean Houle of the Nordiques. "What he did to us, he always has been doing."

They called him Mister Hockey because he meant more to the game than any single player before or since. Now he has passed the puck to his kids and the Howe legend will go on, maybe for another 30 years.

After his "retirement," Howe played an additional two years with the WHA's Houston Aeros.

Norm Ullman, one of the most prolific scorers in NHL history, first as a center with the Detroit Red Wings, and later with the Toronto Maple Leafs, moves in front of Minnesota's Fred Barrett.

*St. Louis Blues and Minnesota
North Stars scramble for the
elusive puck along the side*

*One of the most unusual occurrences in a rink
is the bringing to a halt of Boston's superstar
Bobby Orr. It requires perfect timing and an
abundance of muscle for enemy skaters to
stop the amazing Bobby. The Canadiens do the
trick here as Jacques Lemaire (left) and Serge
Savard (right) apply a pincer squeeze on the
falling Orr while Boston defenseman Dallas
Smith (right) skates in to lend Orr some
assistance.*

217

The panorama of a hockey game. A member of the Soviet National Hockey Team stickhandles the puck at Maple Leaf Gardens in Toronto during the series with Team Canada II in September 1974. Russian skaters, who are offside on the Canadien side of the blue line, race back to center where they will regroup and attempt another attack.

The Rink

The earliest hockey games were played on natural ice without any of the refinements now taken for granted.

The modern rink has been standardized with little flexibility. Most rinks are 200 feet long by 85 feet wide. There are, however, significant exceptions. Chicago Stadium has a rink that is only 188 feet long. Detroit's Olympia Stadium rink is 83 feet wide. Buffalo Memorial Auditorium has a 196 feet long rink. And in Boston the venerable Garden rink is 191 feet by 83 feet.

As a result of these nuances teams are able to devise subtle strategies to capitalize on the quirks of their particular arenas. For years the Red Wings made a practice of arching billiard-like shots off the curiously curved end boards at Olympia Stadium. This produced a familiar (to the Red Wings) ricochet of the puck that baffled visiting teams. In St. Paul the new WHA rink features see-through unbreakable glass sideboards, which frequently confuse opposition skaters.

The perceptive coach, seeking every possible advantage, attempts to make the best possible use of his familiar home rink. Therefore, a club such as the Buffalo Sabres will gear its attack and defense to fit in with the smaller dimensions of Memorial Auditorium.

Likewise, the artificial ice differs in quality and depth from rink to rink. Major arenas such as Madison Square Garden in New York must frequently remove the hockey playing surface to accommodate other attractions—basketball, the circus, musical shows. Because of these changes the Garden ice tends to be vulnerable to constant piercing by the ultra-sharp hockey players' skate blades. Rinks less frequently used by other attractions, such as the Forum in Montreal, are able to retain the ice for longer periods, thereby producing a thicker surface of better quality.

Variations in the rinks, ice and boards notwithstanding hockey remains basically a simple game with one eternal goal—to put the puck in the six foot wide by four foot high net.

219

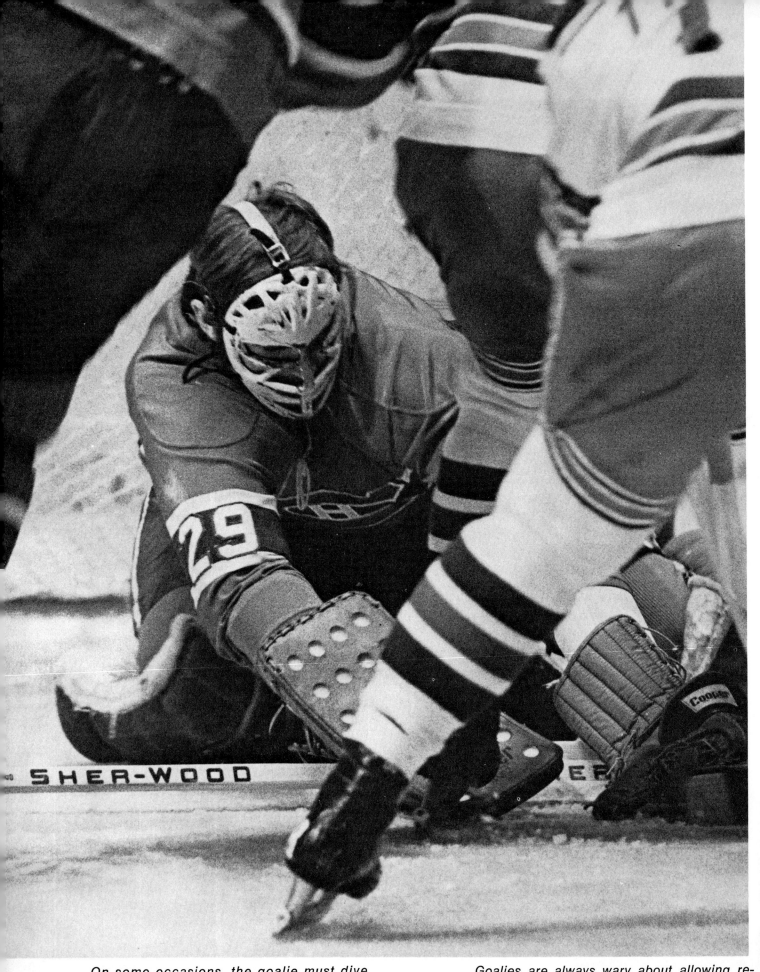

On some occasions, the goalie must dive through a maze of sticks and skates to locate the loose rubber as Ken Dryden does here.

Goalies are always wary about allowing rebounds. The Flyers' Bernie Parent hunches his body over the puck to protect it from the Rangers' forward.

Stan Mikita of the Chicago Black Hawks, here being pursued by the Flyers' Gary Dornhoefer, is a stickhandler supreme among hockey centermen.

Dedications

To everyone who made hockey a joy from day one to the present, and especially my family—Mom, Shirley and Ben, and my all-time favorite photographer, Danny.

S.F.

In the course of engaging in professional photography, a photographer needs assistance of all types. This book is the result of many people's help and understanding. For those who did not help, it is also an indication of what can be done without them.

I am dedicating my portion of this book to Mr. Frank Agolia, a man who helped, understood, and backed many photographers. He was one of the few people who maintained a level of sanity in an often crazy business. He was an inspiration.

I would also like to thank my mother and father for giving me the foundation in life to accomplish so much.

Special thanks to Vin Claps, Harvey Cohen, Scotty Connal, Jerry Cooke, Ed Croke, Joe DiMaggio, Bob Engle, Kevin Fitzgerald, Marty Forscher, Ira Gitler, the Gorillas, Les Gurren, John Halligan, Joe Kadlec, JoAnne Kalish, Sal Marchiano, Ron Meyerson, Ray Ogren, Steve Ross, Tim Ryan, Bill Schaap, Al Szabo, Bill Torrey, and Bob Verdi.

And thanks especially to Stan Fischler, who gave me a start and has continued to work with me.

And to Madeliene, my inspiration.

D.B.

Acknowledgments

All the photos in this book were taken by Dan Baliotti except the following: Page 168, Joe Bongi, Jr.; Page 204, Mike Wesselik; Pages 210, 213, U.P.I.; Page 215, Steve Babineau.

The excerpt from *Working: People Talk About What They Do All Day and How They Feel About What They Do,* by Studs Terkel, copyright 1972, 1974, is reprinted with the permission of Pantheon Books, a Division of Random House, Inc.

Photographic Information

The photographs in color by Dan Baliotti were taken under varying light conditions. Those utilizing available light were shot at either 1/250 second, f/2.8, with 400 ASA tungsten film or at 1/500 second, f/2.8, with ASA 400 daylight film. Other photos were taken using electronic flash equipment (strobe). The strobes were positioned above the rinks to light the entire arena. Film was generally Kodachrome ASA 25, at 1/125 second, f/4 and also Ektachrome ASA 64, at 1/125 second, f/5.6. Lenses ranged from a fisheye (first photo in book) to a 300-mm (photo on page 41). Blurs were obtained using Kodachrome KPA ASA 40, at 1/15 second, f/2.8. The photos showing the scenes from above were taken from catwalks suspended over the ice.

Project Director: Stuart L. Daniels
Art Director: Renate Lude
Associate Art Director: Peter McKenna
Editorial Associate: Daniel Goldschmidt